QUILTING
for the Men in Your Life

Pearl Louise Krush

©2005 Pearl Louise Krush
Published by

kp books
An Imprint of F+W Publications

700 East State Street • Iola, WI 54990-0001
715-445-2214 • 888-457-2873

Library of Congress Catalog Number: 2004098433
ISBN: 0-87349-972-7

Edited by Candy Wiza
Designed by Marilyn McGrane

Printed in the United States of America

Acknowledgments

I would like to thank:

All of the men in my life who, through their various interests, have inspired me with the many design concepts that fill this book.

My husband and best friend, Fred Krush Sr., who, over the years, has taught me to enjoy the many interests he loves so much and who supports all of my creativity.

My acquisitions editor, Julie Stephani, who also is a wonderful, creative friend.

My editor, Candy Wiza, who I have known through the quilt industry for many years and has been so patient and helpful on this project.

My Pearl Louise Designs staff members, Christine Bump and Cynthia Reil, who were so helpful with the making of the projects in this book and with the running of my quilt shop, Thimble Cottage.

A special thank-you to my friend and assistant, Julie Weaver, for all of her diligent help with pulling the projects and this book together.

Table of Contents

Introduction

Creating this book has brought back many thoughts and memories about the wonderful men in my life.

My father was a very clever and creative gentleman. He was a mechanic by trade, but he should have been a mechanical engineer, simply because he had such a natural talent for repairing or building anything mechanical. He was truly an entrepreneur. I know that I have inherited his independent nature and a little of his grand mechanical mind.

My great-grandfather, on my mother's side of the family, taught me how to recycle old materials to make something new. We built my first playhouse together, laying two-by-two lumber pieces in rows, somewhat like building a log cabin. My job was to straighten the used nails.

My husband, Fred, is a great resource for my creativity. Designing quilts in many various themes is a pleasure because of his love of so many sports and hobbies. I also am the mother of three grown sons, and our lives are filled with sports, fishing, hunting and many other masculine interests. Now, I have a very busy 10-year-old grandson who enjoys the same interests as his father, uncles, grandfather and great-grandfather.

My brother is very involved with the hunting and sporting business. He is an excellent taxidermist. I also am blessed with many delightful brothers-in-law. One is developing a small ranch, another is very involved studying astronomy, one is an avid golfer and the others love to hunt and fish.

The many project themes in this book fill the interests of the men in my life and hopefully they will in yours too!

It is often hard to purchase a gift for the men in your life. Creating a quilt, pillow or another project in this book will delight any man. Consider their interests and the style of their home when you choose a project. The projects in the book include pillows, throw quilts, bed quilts and a rug. Set a budget, and decide on the appropriate fabrics for the project you are creating, or the room you are decorating.

Change any of the designs to fit your needs. The instructions for each project are written so each step can be checked off as completed. This will help cut down on cutting and sewing errors. You'll learn iron-on appliqué, strip piecing, rag seams and many other timesaving techniques.

What Makes a Masculine Quilt?

When making projects for the men in your life, consider the many fabric colors, textures and prints available on the market.

If you are planning to use recycled clothing in some of your projects, check the fiber content and washing instructions. Old suits are often available but they are not appropriate for making quilts, as they must be dry cleaned. Wool clothing also is available and can be cut up for quilts, but consider allergies. If the wool is washable, wash it before making the item.

There are tremendous amounts of fabulous fabrics available on the market, with more coming every year. Beautiful batiks, homespun plaids, flannels and wonderful prints fill quilt shops across America.

Fabric Color Choice

The connecting factor in making quilts and other projects for men is choosing fabrics. Most men are involved in something related to nature. So the most natural choice of fabrics for their projects are nature-themed and earth tone fabrics. Darker tones of all fabrics add strength and a quality of richness to the design. The lighter, brighter tones set off both the design and the darker tones in each project.

Medium Colors

Medium shades of earth tone colors such as tan, gray and golden brown add depth to the project designs.

Dark Colors

  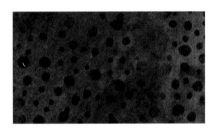

Dark shades of brown, blue, green and black are featured in many of the masculine quilts. These colors add strength to the projects.

Neutral Colors

Cream and beige shades of fabrics create a soft warm background for all of the other colors as they meld and blend with each other. These fabrics highlight the designs on the quilts and other projects.

Warm Colors

 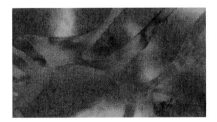 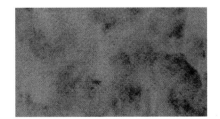

Warm shades of blue, orange, gold and green add warmth and contrast to the darker shades.

Fabric Designs

The various fabrics that simply set a masculine design are rich, textured prints and plaids.

Small, medium and large scale fabrics not only set off each block design, but often become the main

component in both the block and project design.

Small Prints

 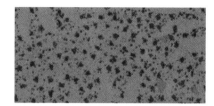 

Small prints are sometimes printed with marble effects, textures and small designs that are not floral. Texture-printed fabrics do not have a lot of different color value or design but still add a rich interest.

Background Prints

The warm background prints that are used for the projects in this book are sometimes tone-on-tone prints that add movement without taking away from the main prints or block designs. Other background ideas are printed fabrics or flannels that highlight the color and design of each block or project component.

Geometric Prints

These prints add spark to a quilt. Sometimes a geometric print can be overpowering to a quilt. Be careful when using too many or too large of a geometric print.

Plaids

There are many plaid fabrics available in cottons, homespuns and flannels. When using plaids, decide if you want to cut on the line (It's a good idea if you are using woven, homespun plaids). In most cases it is not necessary to cut on the printed plaid lines when creat-

ing the pieced blocks, as the overall design will be seen and not the lines on the plaid fabrics. Plaids create a

warm, homey, country and north-woods look when used in quilt making.

Batik Prints

The beauty of batik fabric is the rich coloration of the hand-dyed fabrics. It is recommended to pre-wash this fabric to remove any excess dyes. They are beautiful to work with, and they provide a modern feel to home decorating.

100 Percent Cottons

Flannel

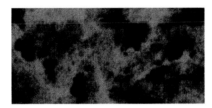

Homespun Flannel

The cotton fabrics available on the market today are made of beautiful, quality material. They are soft and pliable and do not have a heavy sizing or finish. The multitude of designs and prints will fit any theme. They are printed in small, medium and large scales as well as light, medium and dark colors. Always choose quality goods when making any project.

Flannels are 100 percent printed cottons that are brushed on one or both sides. The new quality of flannel is superb. They also are printed with small, medium and large scale designs and simple texture designs. It is recommended that flannel fabric be pre-washed before it is cut. When making the rag edge type of project it is not necessary to pre-wash the flannel fabric.

Homespun flannel is a woven product. It is brushed on one side and not on the other. Both sides can be used for a project. It is best to cut this product on the lines to achieve the straight of grain. Most homespun fabrics are plaids, but recently manufacturers started producing printed homespun fabrics.

Planning

When deciding to make the projects in this book, consider the person you are creating the item for. What is their personality? Where do they live? Look through this book, catalogs and magazines to get a "feeling" for the room setting you desire. If possible, cut and paste a variety of photos in a notebook. Take the notebook with you when you go shopping.

It is also important to set a budget to purchase the fabrics, thread, batting and other accents for the room you are designing.

General Instructions and Tools

Cutting Supplies and Instructions

Cutting instructions are based on 40" to 42" wide, 100 percent cotton fabrics.

¼" seams are used on all pieced and sewn seams unless otherwise stated.

For accurate cutting, a rotary cutter, cutting mat and clear ruler are required.

It is best to check mark each cut, as you complete it, for accuracy.

All seams are sewn with right sides together unless otherwise stated.

All reference to WOF = Width of Fabric.

Sewing Supplies and Instructions

The basic sewing supplies for the projects include:

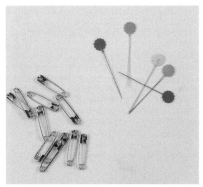

Pins

Flower head pins or silk pins are best for pinning seams before sewing.

1" safety pins are best for pinning the layers of fabrics and batting together before quilting. Pinning is an alternative to thread basting.

Scissors

Good quality scissors are a must for quilt making. Choose a quality, fabric scissors and use it for cutting fabric only.

An all-purpose scissors is used for paper cutting.

A short-blade serrated scissors is used for the clipping on the rag seam quilt and the chenille rug.

A small embroidery scissors is needed for the embroidery technique.

Thread

Use a quality 100 percent cotton thread or poly-wrapped cotton thread for piecing and sewing the projects together.

Use any type of decorative or quality thread for quilting.

DMC® embroidery floss was used on the stitched projects and quilts in this book.

Ironing Board and Iron

An ironing board can be placed at different heights and is very useful. If at all possible, place the ironing board next to your sewing machine table at the same height as the sewing machine table or cabinet.

A clean steam iron is required to press all seams and the iron-on fusible web product.

Press all seams to the dark fabric when possible. Also, press seams that meet, in opposite directions. This allows the seams to "lock" — a technique that aids in accurate piecing.

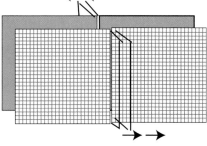

Iron-on Fusible Web

There is a wide assortment of iron-on fusible web products on the market today. The product used for the projects in this book is Steam-a-Seam 2 Lite® from the Warm Company. The basic product consists of a web of glue that is placed between two sheets of paper. Read the manufacturer's instructions provided with the product.

Trace the project appliqués onto the sticky side of the paper. Cut out the appliqué design allowing a ¼" to ½" excess around each shape. Iron the appliqué onto the wrong side of the fabric. Cut out each appliqué fabric on the traced line. Peel off the remaining sheet of paper, arrange the appliqué, and iron in place.

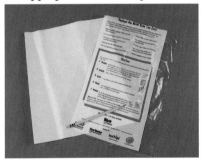

Sewing Machines and Attachments

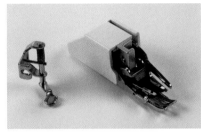

A clean sewing machine in good working condition, that sews a straight stitch, is all that is required for piecing together a quilt.

If you have a machine that does decorative stitches, choose a favorite decorative stitch to sew around each appliqué. The satin and feather stitch were used on some of the appliqué projects in this book.

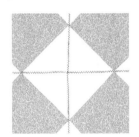

To create meandering or stippling quilting, the feed dogs on the machine need to be in the down position or covered with a protective plate. The attachment for this type of free-form quilting is the darning foot.

The walking foot is another very functional attachment used to machine quilt with the technique known as "stitch in the ditch." The walking foot allows all layers of fabric to be fed through the sewing machine at the same rate of speed — eliminating puckers in the fabric.

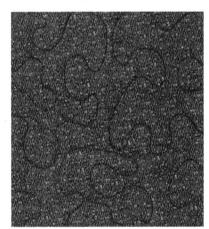

Building Easy Blocks

Many blocks such as half-square triangle blocks, Flying Geese blocks, quarter-square triangle blocks and strip-piecing techniques are repeated throughout this book to build the quilts.

The following diagrams will help with the construction of these blocks.

Half-square triangle blocks

Flying Geese blocks or corner square rectangles

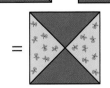

Quarter-square triangle blocks

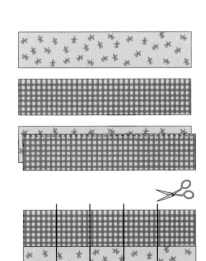

Strip-piecing units

Making Pillows

There are many ways to finish a pillow. Following are two techniques I used in this book.

Pillow technique No. 1

1. Layer the backing, batting and pillow top. Quilt as desired. Cut the shapes to the size required for each project.

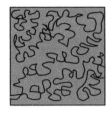

2. Attach the applique (if required) as stated in the instructions.

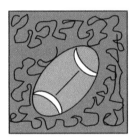

3. Cut the back of the quilted pillow in half. Follow the instructions provided for each pillow.

4. Fold the top edge on each back panel under 1", with wrong sides together, and stitch in place.

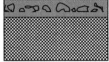

5. Overlap the back panels, with right sides up, and pin in place. Trim the pillow back to the same size as the pillow front.

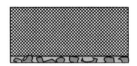

6. With wrong sides together, pin the front and back panels of the pillow together. Trim the edges to fit.

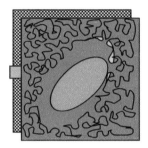

7. Place the binding strips with right sides together. Sew the strips together using diagonal seams. Trim and press.

8. With wrong sides together, fold in half lengthwise and press.

9. Pin the raw edge of the binding to the pillow top raw edges. Sew the binding to the pillow, mitering the corners as shown in the section "Mitering." Insert the pillow form through the section left open (see diagram). Sew the binding in place. Sew the opening closed.

10. Turn the folded edge of the binding to the pillow back. Hand sew in place.

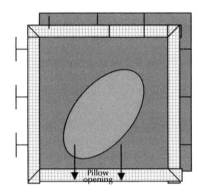

Pillow technique No. 2

1. Match the pillow front and back with wrong sides together.

2. Pin and sew the raw edge of the binding to the outer edge of the pillow, connecting the front and back panels. Leave a small space open for stuffing.

3. Pin the raw edge of the binding to the front edge on the pillow panel on the opening. Stuff the pillow, and carefully continue sewing the binding.

4. Turn the binding to the back, and hand sew the folded edge of the binding in place.

Mitering

1. Beginning on one side of the quilt (not on the corner) align the raw edges of the binding along the quilt top edge.

2. Pin the binding to the quilt, leaving a 6" tail.

3. Sew ¼" from the edge. To miter corners as you sew, stop sewing ¼" from the corner. Remove the quilt from under the machine. Fold the binding at a 45-degree angle, up and away from the quilt as shown.

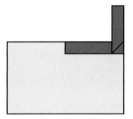

4. Fold the binding back down, even with the raw edge, and continue sewing the binding in place.

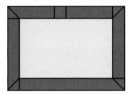

5. When you are close to the original starting point, overlap the bindings about 4" and cut off the excess.

6. Cut the binding to match the angle of the original tail. Fold under ¼" and press. Place the raw edges of the tail inside the folded edges. Hem stitch the ends together.

7. Turn the folded edge of the binding to the back and hand sew in place.

The measurements for borders are not usually stated in this book. The top and bottom borders are determined by measuring horizontally across the center of the quilt. Measure the quilt vertically down the center, from top to bottom, to get the side border measurements.

Embroidery Stitches

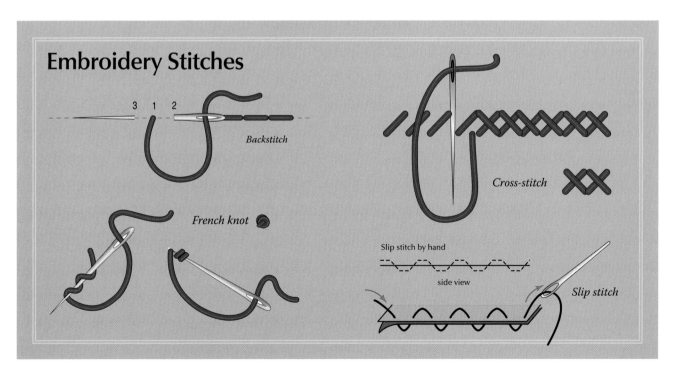

3 1 2

Backstitch

French knot

Cross-stitch

Slip stitch by hand

side view

Slip stitch

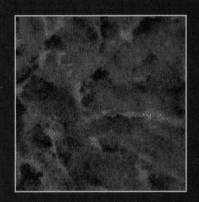

CHAPTER 1

A Gentleman's Haven

Cuddle under this rich and colorful flannel collection that has the look of fine-textured leather. The quilt is easy to make and will look great in any office, den or bedroom. The coordinating wall hanging and pillow in this set add the finishing touch.

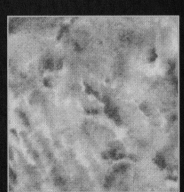

A Gentleman's Haven
QUILT

This quilt is one of the easiest quilts to construct. Handmade in rich colorful flannels, A Gentleman's Haven conveys the illusion of royalty. Take advantage of its manly size and warmth while reading your favorite novel or taking a long leisurely nap.

Finished size: 63" x 81"

Fabrics and Notions

- 2 yd. cream marble-print flannel (blocks)
- 1½ yd. brown marble-print flannel (blocks, binding)
- 1 yd. rust marble-print flannel (blocks)
- 1 yd. green marble-print flannel (blocks)
- 1 yd. gold marble-print flannel (blocks)
- 5 yd. flannel for backing
- Full-size batting (81" x 96")
- Matching thread

Tools and Supplies

- Basic sewing supplies
- Rotary cutter
- Cutting mat
- Clear ruler

Cutting Instructions

From the cream marble-print flannel, cut:
- (16) 3½" x WOF strips
  From these strips, cut: (63) 3½" x 9½" rectangles

From the brown marble-print flannel, cut:
- (8) 3½" x WOF strips
  From these strips, cut: (32) 3½" x 9½" rectangles
- (9) 2½" x WOF strips

From the rust marble-print flannel, cut:
- (8) 3½" x WOF strips
  From these strips, cut: (31) 3½" x 9½" rectangles

From the green marble-print flannel, cut:
- (8) 3½" x WOF Strips
  From these strips, cut: (31) 3½" x 9½" rectangles

From the gold marble-print flannel, cut:
- (8) 3½" x WOF strips
  From these strips, cut: (32) 3½" x 9½" rectangles

Preparation

1. Read all instructions before you begin.

2. Wash, dry and press all fabrics.

3. Cutting instructions are based on 40" wide fabrics. WOF = Width of Fabric.

4. Use ¼" seams throughout.

5. Press seam allowances in the direction that allows the seams to "lock" before continuing to build each block.

6. Press all seams to the dark fabric when possible.

Build the Rail Fence Blocks

Make 32 cream/brown/gold 9½" blocks.

Refer to the block layout.

1. With right sides together, sew a 3½" x 9½" cream rectangle to a 3½" x 9½" brown rectangle along the 9½" side.

2. Sew a gold 3½" x 9½" rectangle to the brown rectangle along the 9½" side. Repeat to make a total of 32 Rail Fence blocks.

3. Press each block.

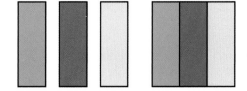

Make 31 cream/rust/green 9½" blocks.

1. With right sides together, sew a 3½" x 9½" cream rectangle to a rust 3½" x 9½" rectangle along the 9½" side.

2. Sew a 3½" x 9½" green rectangle to the rust rectangle along the 9½". Repeat to make a total of 31 Rail Fence blocks.

3. Press each block.

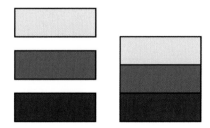

Build the Quilt

Refer to the quilt layout photo.

1. With right sides together, sew seven blocks together to make each row. Make nine rows. Press.

2. With right sides together, sew the nine rows together. Press.

Finish the Quilt

Refer to the General Instructions for mitering bindings on page 13.

1. With right sides together, sew the backing fabric lengths together. Press.

2. Layer the backing (face down), batting and quilt top (face up). Baste and quilt as desired. The model was quilted using an overall meander quilting technique.

3. Sew the brown 2½" binding strips, with right sides together, end to end. Fold in half lengthwise with wrong sides together. Press.

4. Pin the raw edge of the binding to the outer edge of the quilt top. Sew the binding to the quilt top ¼" from the edge, mitering the corners as the binding is attached.

5. Trim the fabric backing and batting to within ¼" around the entire quilt.

6. Turn the folded edge of the binding to the back of the quilt. Hand or machine sew in place.

A Gentleman's Haven
PILLOW

The rich, textured flannel, resembling fine leather, is a fabulous cover for this wonderful over-sized pillow. Prepared with the same Rail Fence blocks that were used for the coordinating quilt, it's a great addition on an easy chair, couch or bed.

Finished size: 18" square

Preparation

1. Read all instructions before you begin.

2. Wash, dry and press all fabrics.

3. Cutting instructions are based on 40" wide fabrics. WOF = Width of Fabric.

4. Use ¼" seams throughout.

5. Press seam allowances in the direction that allows the seams to "lock" before continuing to build each block.

6. Press all seams to the dark fabric when possible.

Make the Rail Fence Blocks

Refer to the block layout.

Make four cream/brown/gold 9½" blocks.

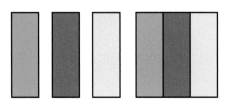

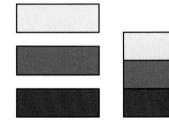

Make four cream/rust/green 9½" blocks.

1. With right sides together, sew a 3½" x 9½" cream rectangle to a 3½" x 9½" brown rectangle along the 9½" side. Sew a gold 3½" x 9½" rectangle to the brown rectangle along the 9½" side. Repeat to make a total of four Rail Fence blocks.

2. With right sides together, sew a 3½" x 9½" cream rectangle to a rust 3½" x 9½" rectangle along the 9½" side. Sew a 3½" x 9½" green rectangle to the rust rectangle along the 9½" side. Repeat to make a total of four blocks.

3. Press each block.

Fabrics and Notions

- ⅓ yd. cream marble-print flannel (blocks)
- ⅓ yd. brown marble-print flannel (blocks, binding)
- ⅛ yd. rust marble-print flannel (blocks)
- ⅛ yd. green marble-print flannel (blocks)
- ⅛ yd. gold marble-print flannel (blocks)
- 1½ yd. muslin
- 1½ yd. batting
- 18" pillow form or poly fill
- Matching thread

Tools and Supplies

- Basic sewing supplies
- Rotary cutter
- Cutting mat
- Clear ruler

Cutting Instructions

From the cream marble-print flannel, cut:
- (2) 3½" x WOF strips
  From these strips, cut: (8) 3½" x 9½" rectangles

From the rust marble-print flannel, cut:
- (1) 3½" x WOF strip
  From this strip, cut: (4) 3½" x 9½" rectangles

From the green marble-print flannel, cut:
- (1) 3½" x WOF strip
  From this strip, cut: (4) 3½" x 9½" rectangles

From the gold marble-print flannel, cut:
- (1) 3½" x WOF strips
  From this strip, cut: (4) 3½" x 9½" rectangles

From the brown marble-print flannel, cut:
- (1) 3½ " x WOF strip
  From this strip, cut: (4) 3½" x 9½" rectangles
- (2) 2½" x WOF strips

From the muslin, cut:
- (2) 22" squares

From the batting, cut:
- (2) 22" squares

Make the Pillow

Refer to the pillow layout and the General Instructions for mitering bindings on page 13.

1. With right sides together, sew two sets (pillow front and back) of four blocks. Press.

 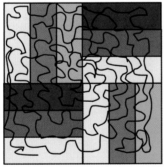

2. Layer the muslin, batting and pillow front (face up). Repeat for the pillow back.

3. Baste and quilt the pillow front and back as desired. The model was quilted with an overall meander quilting technique.

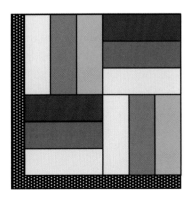

4. Trim the batting and muslin to the edge of the blocks.

5. Match the front and back of the pillow with wrong sides together. Pin to secure.

6. Sew the 2½" binding strips, with right sides together, end to end. Press. Fold in half lengthwise with wrong sides together. Press.

7. Pin and sew the raw edge of the binding to the outer edge of the pillow, connecting the front and back panels. Miter the corners. Leave an opening at the bottom of the pillow for stuffing.

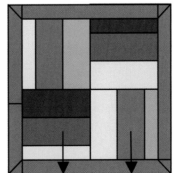

8. Pin the binding to the top pillow layer, between the opening. Insert the pillow form or poly fill. Continue sewing the binding in place on the open area.

9. Turn the folded edge of the binding to the back. Hand sew in place.

Rolling Hills
WALL QUILT

This wall quilt adds an inspirational dimension to a wall in an office, library or bedroom. The lazy rolling hills, lake and sky suggest a landscape theme, creating a soothing piece of artwork. The flannel appliqués tend to adhere to themselves and the background fabric, so there isn't any need to use iron-on fusible web. Simply pin and stitch the appliqués in place.

Finished size: 26" x 36"

Preparation

1. Read all instructions before you begin.

2. Wash, dry and press all fabrics.

3. Cutting instructions are based on 40" wide fabrics. WOF = Width of Fabric.

4. Use ¼" seams throughout.

5. Press seam allowances in the direction that allows the seams to "lock" before continuing to build each block.

6. Press all seams to the dark fabric when possible.

Build the Wall Quilt

1. Lay out the rolling hills on the cream background as shown on the photo. Start placing the hills from the bottom of the wall quilt. Arrange each hill until the design is pleasing. Pin in place. (There is no need to use iron-on fusible web for this project because the flannel appliqués tend to adhere to each other.) Trim the hill appliqués to the background.

2. With right sides together, sew the 3½" x 20½" brown border strips to the top and bottom of the center panel. Sew the 3½" x 36½" borders to the sides of the quilt.

3. Sew around each hill appliqué using decorative stitches. The model was sewn using blanket stitches and tan thread.

Step 2. *Sew the brown border strips to the center panel.*

Fabrics and Notions

- ⅔ yd. tan marble-print flannel (background)
- Fat quarter green marble-print flannel (hills)
- Fat quarter rust marble-print flannel (hills)
- Fat quarter tan marble-print flannel (hills)
- 1 yd. brown marble-print flannel (hills, binding)
- 1 yd. backing flannel
- Hill patterns from the pattern insert
- 1 yd. batting
- 1 yd. iron-on fusible web (if desired)
- 3 "O" ½" rings for hanging
- Matching thread

Tools and Supplies

- Basic sewing supplies
- Rotary cutter
- Cutting mat
- Clear ruler

Cutting Instructions

From the cream marble-print flannel, cut:
- (1) 20½" x 30½" rectangle

From the brown marble-print flannel, cut:
- (2) 3½" x 36½" border strips
- (2) 3½" x 20½" border strips
- (3) 2½" x WOF strips
- (3) hills from the pattern insert

From the tan marble-print flannel, cut:
- (4) hills from the pattern insert

From the rust marble-print flannel, cut:
- (3) hills from the pattern insert

From the green marble-print flannel, cut:
- (4) hills from the pattern insert

From the backing flannel, cut:
- (1) 30" x 40" rectangle

From the batting, cut:
- (1) 30" x 40" rectangle

Finish the Wall Quilt

Refer to the General Instructions for mitering bindings on page 13.

1. Layer the backing (face down), batting and quilt top (face up). Pin or baste. Quilt as desired. The model was quilted using an overall meander quilting technique.

2. Sew the 2½" binding strips, with right sides together, end to end. Fold in half lengthwise with wrong sides together. Press.

3. Pin the binding to the quilt, matching raw edges. Sew the binding to the outer edge of the quilt top. Miter the corners as the binding is attached.

4. Trim the batting and backing fabrics, leaving a ¼" seam allowance around the entire quilt.

5. Turn the folded edge of the binding to the back. Hand sew in place.

6. Sew ½" "O" rings to the back top of the quilt for hanging.

CHAPTER 2

Touchdown

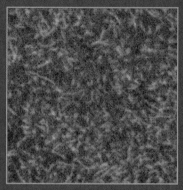

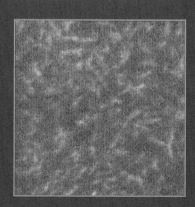

Enjoy those crisp, fall evenings as you cuddle up in this quick and easy-to-make throw quilt. You definitely will score big with any guy wanting to watch his team race down the football field to make another touchdown. The tote in this collection allows for easy travel and the pillow adds a touch of comfort. The perfect collection for a tailgate party!

The Touchdown
THROW QUILT

Strip-piecing, iron-on appliqué and easy-to-sew flannel prints make this quilt a breeze to make. The football quilt is a great car quilt or one to warm the bench while you watch your favorite ball game. Every fan and player will love this special quilt.

Finished size: 66½" x 76"

Fabrics and Notions

- 1⅓ yd. No. 1 green print flannel (center)
- 1¾ yd. No. 2 green print flannel (border)
- ¾ yd. cream print flannel (grid lines, inner border)
- ¼ yd. rust print flannel (footballs, border corner squares)
- 1¼ yd. rust plaid flannel (outer border, binding)
- 4 yd. plaid backing flannel
- Football and football band patterns from the pattern insert
- 4 yd. batting
- 1 yd. iron-on fusible web
- 1 skein cream/white embroidery floss
- Rust-colored thread
- Cream-colored thread

Tools and Supplies

- Basic sewing supplies
- Rotary cutter
- Cutting mat
- Clear ruler

Cutting Instructions

From the No. 1 green print flannel, cut:
- (5) 8½" x 40½" strips

From the No. 2 green print flannel, cut:
- (7) 8½" x WOF strips

From the cream print flannel, cut:
- (6) 2½" x 40½" strips
- (3) 2½" x WOF strips
- (3) football band appliqués from "fused" flannel

From the rust print flannel, cut:
- (4) 2½" squares
- (3) football appliqués from "fused" flannel

From the rust print flannel, cut:
- (8) 2½" x WOF strips
- (8) 2½" x WOF strips (binding)

From the backing flannel, cut:
- (2) 42" x 72" pieces

Note: See the directions for fusing the fabric.

Preparation

1. Read all instructions before you begin.

2. Wash, dry and press all fabrics.

3. Cutting instructions are based on 40" wide fabrics. WOF = Width of Fabric.

4. Use ¼" seams throughout.

5. Press seam allowances in the direction that allows the seams to "lock" before continuing to build each block.

6. Press all seams to the dark fabric when possible.

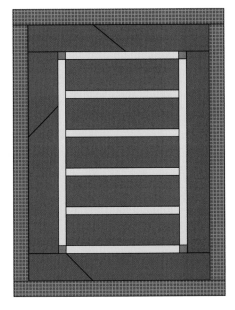

Build the Quilt

Refer to the quilt photo.

1. With right sides together, sew a 2½" x 40½" cream strip to the top edge of the five 8½" x 40½" No. 1 green strips. Press.

2. Sew the five rows together with right sides together. Press.

3. Sew a 2½" x 40½" cream strip, with right sides together, to the bottom of the cream/green strip.

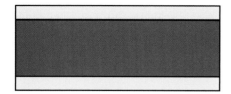

4. Sew the 2½" x WOF cream border strips, with right sides together, to measure 48½". Make two.

5. Sew a 2½" rust square, with right sides together, to the ends of the 2½" x 48½" cream side borders.

6. Sew the cream side borders, with right sides together, to the center panel. Press.

7. Piece and sew the No. 2 green 8½" x WOF border strips with right sides together. Measure the quilt sides to determine the length of the border strips. Cut the border strips to match. Sew the side border strips to the center with right sides together. Sew the top and bottom borders, with right sides together, to the quilt center.

8. Piece and sew the rust plaid 2½" x WOF border strips with right sides together. Measure the quilt sides to determine the length of the border strips. Cut the border strips. Sew the side border strips to the center with right sides together, Sew the top and bottom borders, with right sides together, to the quilt center. Press.

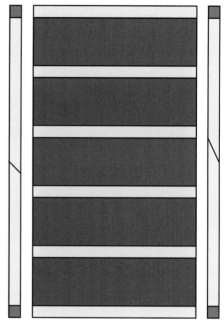

Make the Football Appliqués

1. Cut out the football and football bands from the pattern insert. Trace three footballs and six football bands onto the paper layer of the iron-on fusible web, allowing ½" between each shape. Cut out the shapes. Follow the manufacturer's directions for using fusible web.

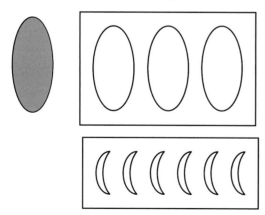

2. Remove the paper backing. Iron the sticky side of the fusible web to the wrong side of the appliqué fabrics. Cut out each shape.

3. Remove the paper backing and place the football shapes where desired.

4. Iron the football bands onto each football. Iron the football appliqués onto the quilt.

5. Use a ruler and pencil to draw a 4" line on the center on each football 1" inside the cream print bands. Draw a 4" line on each side of the centerline.

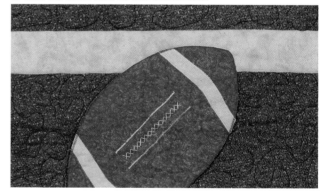

6. Use rust-colored thread to satin stitch around each football. Use cream-colored thread to satin stitch around the football bands. Satin stitch the straight side lines on each football. Refer to the football appliqué photo.

7. Use four strands of cream/white embroidery floss to cross-stitch the center seam on each football.

Finish the Quilt

1. Sew the two backing fabric pieces with right sides together.

2. Layer the backing (face down), batting and quilt top (face up). Baste and quilt as desired. A medium meander quilting technique was used on the sample quilt.

3. Sew the rust plaid binding strips, with right sides together, end to end. Fold in half lengthwise with wrong sides together. Press.

4. Sew the raw edge of the binding to the outer edge of the quilt top.

5. Trim the fabric backing and batting, leaving a ¼" seam allowance.

6. Turn the folded edge of the binding to the back of the quilt. Hand sew in place.

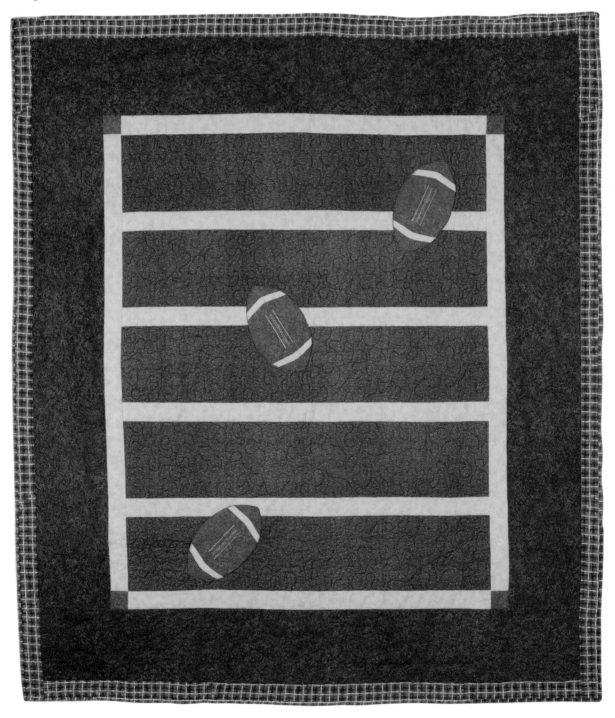

The Touchdown
TOTE

This handy tote is oh-so-easy to make, you'll want to make several to give as gifts. The lining and body of the tote sew together in no time and the football appliqué adds a sporty accent. The quilt easily fits into the bag for taking to the game.

Finished size: 12" square

Fabrics and Notions

- 1½ yd. green print flannel (tote, lining)
- ½ yd. rust plaid (handle, binding)
- Fat quarter rust print (football appliqué)
- Scrap cream print flannel (football band)
- Football and football band patterns from the pattern insert
- 1 yd. muslin
- 1 yd. batting
- ¼ yd. iron-on fusible web
- 1 skein cream/white embroidery floss
- Rust-colored thread
- Cream-colored thread

Tools and Supplies

- Basic sewing supplies
- Rotary cutter
- Cutting mat
- Clear ruler

Cutting Instructions

From the green print flannel, cut:
- (2) 14½" squares (tote front and back)
- (3) 6½" x 14½" rectangles (sides and bottom)
- (2) 11½" x 13" squares (pocket front and back)
- (3) 4½" x 12½" rectangles (side and bottom linings)
- (2) 11½" x 13" squares (front and back linings)

From the muslin, cut:
- (2) 14½" squares (quilting foundations)
- (3) 6½" x 14½" rectangles (quilting foundations)

From the rust print flannel, cut:
- (1) football from "fused" flannel

From the cream print flannel, cut:
- (2) football bands from "fused" flannel

From the rust plaid flannel, cut:
- (2) 2½" x WOF strips for binding
- (1) 6½" x 30½" rectangle for handle

From the batting, cut:
- (2) 14½" squares (tote front and back)
- (1) 11½" x 13" rectangle (pocket)
- (3) 6½" x 14½" rectangles (sides and bottom)
- (1) 2½" x 30½" rectangle (handle)

Note: See the directions for fusing the fabrics.

Preparation

1. Read all instructions before you begin.

2. Wash, dry and press all fabrics.

3. Cutting instructions are based on 40" wide fabrics. WOF = Width of Fabric.

4. Use ¼" seams throughout.

5. Press seam allowances in the direction that allows the seams to "lock" before continuing to build each block.

6. Press all seams to the dark fabric when possible.

Build the Tote

1. Tote front and back: Layer the 14½" squares of muslin, batting and green print flannel (face up). Pin or baste.

2. Sides and bottom: Layer the 6½" x 14½" rectangles of muslin, batting and green flannel (face up). Pin or baste.

3. Quilt as desired. Small meander quilting was used on the sample.

4. Pocket: Layer the 11½" x 13" rectangles of green print (face down), batting and green print (face up). Pin or baste.

5. Quilt as desired. Small meander quilting was used on the sample.

6. Cut the quilted tote front and back 14½" squares into two 12½" squares. Cut the quilted pocket 11½" x 13" rectangle into a 10½" x 12½" rectangle. Cut the quilted sides and bottom 6½" x 14½" rectangles to 4½" x 12½".

7. Sew the rust plaid 2½" x WOF binding strips, with right sides together, end to end. Fold in half lengthwise with wrong sides together. Press.

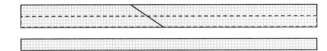

8. Make the pocket: Sew the raw edge on the binding to one 12½" edge on the quilted 10½" x 12½" rectangle. Turn the folded edge of the binding to the inside. Hand sew in place. Set aside the remaining binding.

Make the Football Appliqué

1. Cut out the football and football bands from the pattern insert. Trace one football and two football bands onto the paper layer of the iron-on fusible web, allowing ½" between each shape. Cut out the shapes. Follow the manufacturer's directions for using the fusible web.

2. Remove the paper backing. Iron the sticky side of the fusible web to the wrong side of the appliqué fabrics. Cut out each shape.

3. Remove the paper backing and place the football shape on the pocket center. Iron in place.

4. Iron the football bands onto the football.

5. Use a ruler and pencil to draw a 4" line on the center on each football 1" inside the cream bands. Draw a 4" line on each side of the centerline.

6. Use rust-colored thread to satin stitch around each football. Use cream-colored thread to satin stitch around the football bands. Satin stitch the straight side lines on each football. Refer to the football appliqué photo.

7. Use four strands of cream/white embroidery floss to cross-stitch the center seam on each football.

Sew the Tote

1. Pin the wrong side of the bound pocket onto the right side of one 12½" quilted panel, with the bottom raw edges meeting. Sew together along both 12½" side edges.

2. Pin a quilted 4½" x 12½" green rectangle, with right sides together, on one side of the 12½" quilted square back panel. Sew the 12½" seam.

3. With right sides together, pin and sew a quilted green 4½" x 12½" rectangle to the opposite side of the 12½" back panel edge.

4. With right sides together, pin and sew one 12½" side of the pocket tote front to one 12½" side panel.

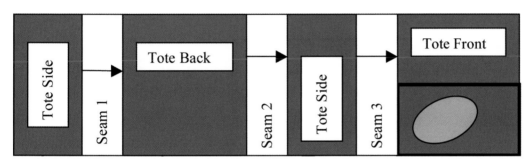

5. Sew the bottom unit to the tote: Pin the 4½" side of the bottom, right sides together, on the 4½" edge of the side panel. Sew in place. Leave the needle inserted.

6. Rotate and sew the bottom 12½" back panel, with right sides together, to the 12½" edge of the bottom panel. Leave the needle inserted.

7. Rotate and sew the 4½" bottom panel edge to the 4½" side panel. Leave the needle inserted.

8. Rotate and sew the 12½" bottom panel edge to the 12½" tote front bottom edge.

9. Lift the needle. Place the 12½" sides of the side panel and tote front, right sides together, and sew together.

10. Turn right-side out.

11. Sew the tote lining following Steps 2 through 9. Do not turn right-side out. Place the tote lining inside the body of the tote.

12. Place the raw edge of the binding on the top edge of the tote. Pin in place, connecting the lining, tote body and binding. Sew around the tote, overlapping the binding ends. Turn the folded edge of the binding to the inside. Hand sew in place.

13. Fold one long edge on the tote handle fabric ½" to the wrong side. Press.

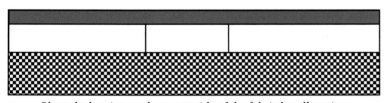

Place the batting on the wrong side of the fabric handle strip.

Fold fabric to the center.

14. Place the batting strip down the center on the wrong side of the tote handle fabric strip. Fold the sides of the handle fabric to the center, with the folded edge over the raw edge. Pin and sew in place.

15. Fold the short ends of the handle over ½", with right sides together, and topstitch.

16. Pin the handle to the inside top edges on each side of the tote. Match the folded edge to the lining. Sew the handle ends in place.

The Touchdown
PILLOW

Throw this pillow in the car and you will have a touch of comfort when napping between games. Quilt the front and back of the pillow before adding the appliqué.

Finished size: 12" square

Preparation

1. Read all instructions before you begin.

2. Wash, dry and press all fabrics.

3. Cutting instructions are based on 40" wide fabrics. WOF = Width of Fabric.

4. Use ¼" seams throughout.

5. Press seam allowances in the direction that allows the seams to "lock" before continuing to build each block.

6. Press all seams to the dark fabric when possible.

Make the Pillow

Refer to the General Instructions for making pillows on pages 12 and 13.

Pillow Front and Back
1. Layer the 14½" squares of muslin, batting and green print (face up). Baste and quilt as desired. A medium, meander quilting technique was used on the sample.

2. Trim one of the quilted squares (front) to measure 12½" square.

Fabrics and Notions

- ½ yd. green print flannel (pillow back and front)
- Fat quarter rust print flannel (football appliqué)
- Scrap cream print flannel (football bands)
- ¼ yd. rust plaid flannel (binding)
- Football and football band from the pattern insert
- ½ yd. muslin
- ½ yd. batting
- ¼ yd. iron-on fusible web
- 12"-14" pillow form
- 1 skein cream/white embroidery floss
- Rust-colored thread
- Cream-colored thread

Tools and Supplies

- Basic sewing supplies
- Rotary cutter
- Cutting mat
- Clear ruler
- Pencil

Cutting Instructions

From the green print flannel, cut:
- (2) 14½" squares

From the muslin, cut:
- (2) 14½" squares

From the batting, cut:
- (2) 14½" squares

From the rust plaid flannel, cut:
- (2) 2½" x WOF strips for binding

From the rust print flannel, cut:
- (1) "fused" football

From the cream scrap flannel, cut:
- (2) "fused" football bands

Note: See the directions for fusing the fabric.

Make the Football Appliqué

1. Cut out the football and football bands from the pattern insert. Trace one football and two football bands onto the paper layer of the iron-on fusible web, allowing ½" between each shape. Cut out the shapes. Follow the manufacturer's directions for using fusible web.

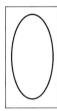

2. Remove the paper backing. Iron the sticky side of the fusible web to the wrong side of the appliqué fabrics. Cut out each shape.

3. Remove the paper backing and place the football shape onto the center front of the 12½" square. Iron in place.

4. Iron the football bands onto the football.

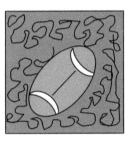

5. Use a ruler and pencil to draw a 4" line on the center on each football 1" inside the cream print bands. Draw a 4" line on each side of the centerline.

6. Use rust-colored thread to satin stitch around the football. Use cream-colored thread to satin stitch around the football bands. Satin stitch the straight side lines on each football. Refer to the football appliqué photo.

7. Use four strands of cream/white embroidery floss to cross-stitch the center seam on each football.

Finish the Pillow

Refer to the General Instructions for mitering bindings on page 13.

1. Cut the remaining (back) quilted green print 14½" square in half to measure two 7¼" x 14½" rectangles.

2. Sew the rust plaid binding strips, with right sides together, end to end. Fold in half lengthwise, wrong sides together, and press.

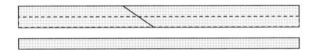

3. Sew the raw edge of the binding to the right side of one 14½" top edge on each of the two 7¼" x 14½" rectangles.

4. Turn the folded edge of the binding to the back on both pieces. Hand sew in place.

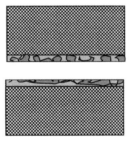

5. Place the two back pieces right-side up. Overlap the two bound edges about 1½". Pin to secure. Cut into a 12½" square.

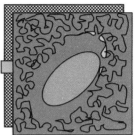

6. Place the pillow front and back with wrong sides together. Trim the edges to fit.

7. Pin the raw edge of the rust plaid binding around the outer top edge of the pillow. Sew the binding in place, mitering the corners as you sew. Overlap the ends.

8. Turn the folded edge of the binding to the back of the pillow. Hand sew in place.

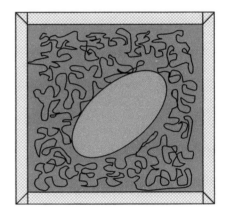

9. Insert the pillow form through the envelope back.

CHAPTER 3

Goal Tenders

Decorate a guest room or a boy's room using this collection of soccer-themed projects. The easy, pieced quilt is accented with the coordinating appliquéd pillow and pennant valance. Crisp colors of black, red, white, cream and gray add a tailored touch to the collection. Decorative machine stitches set off each block on the quilt.

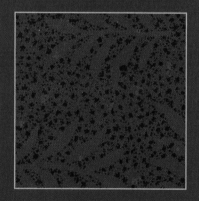

Goal Tender
THROW QUILT

What soccer enthusiast wouldn't love to own this classic quilt. For a simple variation, apply the appliqué soccer ball and motifs from the pillow project, and you'll delight any true soccer fan.

Finished size: 66" x 76"

Fabrics and Notions

- 3 yd. assorted cream and white prints (center squares)
- 3½ yd. gray print (center squares)
- 1½ yd. red print (inner border, binding)
- ⅛ yd. black print (cornerstone squares)
- 1¼ yd. charcoal print (outer border)
- 4 yd. backing fabric
- Twin-size batting (72" x 90")
- Matching thread

Tools and Supplies

- Basic sewing supplies
- Rotary cutter
- Cutting mat
- Clear ruler

Cutting Instructions

From the white/cream print, cut:
- (17) 5½" x WOF strips
  From these strips, cut: (116) 5½" squares
- (2) 5⅞" squares

From the gray print, cut:
- (7) 10½" x WOF strips
  From these strips, cut: (20) 10½" squares
- (6) 5½" x WOF Strips
  From these strips, cut: (18) 5½" x 10½" rectangles
- (1) 5⅞" x WOF strip
  From this strip, cut: (2) 5⅞" squares

From the red print, cut:
- (7) 3½" x WOF strips (inner border)
- (8) 2½" x WOF strips (binding)

From the black print, cut:
- (1) 3½" x WOF strip
  From this strip, cut: (4) 3½" squares

From the charcoal print, cut:
- (7) 5½" x WOF strips (outer border)

Preparation

1. Read all instructions before you begin.

2. Wash, dry and press all fabrics.

3. Cutting instructions are based on 40" wide fabrics. WOF = Width of Fabric.

4. Use ¼" seams throughout.

5. Press seam allowances in the direction that allows the seams to "lock" before continuing to build each block.

6. Press all seams to the dark fabric when possible.

Make the Square-in-a-Square Blocks

Make (20) 10½" blocks

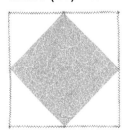

1. Draw a diagonal line across the wrong side on the 116 cream/white 5½" squares and the two 5⅞" cream/white squares. Eighty of the 5½" cream/white squares will be used in the 20 square-in-a-square blocks.

2. Place a drawn-on 5½" cream/white square, with right sides together, on the upper right corner and the lower left corner on a 10½" gray square. Sew on the drawn line. Trim, leaving a ¼" seam. Open and press.

3. Repeat Step 2 on the upper left and lower right side on the 10½" gray square. Trim, open and press.

4. Make a total of 20 blocks.

Make the Flying Geese Blocks
Make (18) 5½" x 10½" blocks.

1. Place a drawn-on 5½" cream/white square, with right sides together, on the **right** side of the 5½" x 10½" gray rectangle. Sew on the drawn line. Trim, leaving a ¼" seam. Open and press.

2. Repeat Step 1 on the **left** side of each 5½" x 10½" gray rectangle.

3. Make a total of 18 blocks.

Make the Half-Square Triangle Blocks
Make (4) 5½" blocks.

1. Draw a diagonal line on the wrong side of the 5⅞" cream/white squares.

2. Place the drawn-on squares, with right sides together, on the 5⅞" gray squares.

3. Sew a ¼" seam on each side of the drawn line.

4. Cut apart on the drawn line.

5. Open and press.

6. Make a total of four blocks.

Build the Quilt
Refer to the block layout diagram.

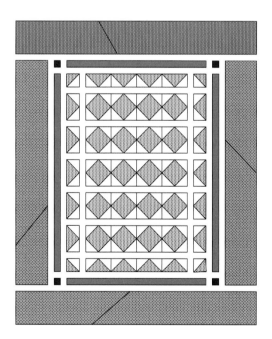

1. Lay out the blocks as shown. All the pieces are sewn with right sides together.

2. Sew four of the square-in-a-square blocks together to make each row.

3. Make five rows.

4. Sew a Flying Geese block to the right side and left side on each row.

5. Sew two rows of four Flying Geese blocks together to make the top and bottom rows.

6. Sew a half-square triangle block to the ends of the top and bottom rows of the Flying Geese blocks.

7. Sew the five rows of square-in-a-square blocks and Flying Geese blocks together. Press.

8. Sew the Flying Geese block top and bottom rows to the top and bottom of the quilt center. Press.

9. Sew the red inner border strips to the sides of the quilt. Press.

10. Sew the black print cornerstone squares to the ends of the top and bottom red border strips. Press.

11. Sew the top and bottom red borders to the quilt. Press.

12. Piece and sew the charcoal border strips, with right sides together, end to end. Measure the quilt sides. Cut the correct lengths of charcoal border strips.

13. Sew the charcoal borders to the sides of the quilt. Press. Sew the top and bottom borders to the quilt. Press.

14. Layer the backing (face down), batting and quilt top (face up). Baste and quilt as desired. In the sample shown, all blocks were defined by machine stitching a black decorative feather stitch around each block. Each block and border were quilted with coordinating threads and a medium meander quilting technique.

15. Sew the red binding strips, with right sides together, end to end. Fold in half lengthwise with wrong sides together. Press.

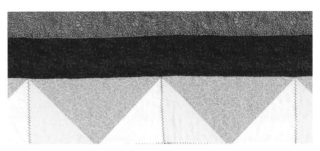

Pin and sew borders in place.

16. Pin and sew the raw edge of the binding to the outer edge of the quilt top mitering the corners as you attach the binding.

17. Trim the backing fabric and batting, leaving a ¼" seam allowance.

18. Turn the folded edge of the binding to the back of the quilt. Hand sew in place.

PILLOW

This easy-to-make pillow is the perfect accent for the soccer collection. Iron-on appliqué shapes create the soccer ball motif.

Finished size: 12" square

Fabrics and Notions

- ½ yd. charcoal print (pillow back and front)
- Fat quarter cream/white print (soccer ball)
- ⅛ yd. white print (soccer ball motifs)
- ⅛ yd. black print (soccer ball motifs)
- ¼ yd. red print (binding)
- Soccer patterns from the pattern insert
- ½ yd. muslin (quilting foundation)
- ½ yd. batting
- ⅔ yd. iron-on fusible web
- 12"-14" pillow form
- Matching thread

Tools and Supplies

- Basic sewing supplies
- Rotary cutter
- Cutting mat
- Clear ruler

Cutting Instructions

From the charcoal print, cut:
- (2) 14½" squares

From the red print, cut:
- (2) 2½" binding strips

From the muslin, cut:
- (2) 14½" squares

From the batting, cut:
- (2) 14½" squares

Preparation

1. Read all instructions before you begin.

2. Wash, dry and press all fabrics.

3. Cutting instructions are based on 40" wide fabrics. WOF = Width of Fabric.

4. Use ¼" seams throughout.

5. Press seam allowances in the direction that allows the seams to "lock" before continuing to build each block.

6. Press all seams to the dark fabric when possible.

Quilt the Pillow Top and Back

1. Layer the 14½" squares of muslin, batting and charcoal print (face up) to make the pillow front and back.

2. Baste and quilt as desired. An overall small meander quilting technique was used on the model.

Build the Pillow

Refer to the General Instructions for making pillows on pages 12 and 13.

Soccer Appliqués

1. Cut out the soccer ball and soccer motifs from the pattern insert.

2. Trace the ball and the nine motifs on the paper side of the iron-on fusible web paper. Cut out each shape allowing ½" excess around each shape. Follow the manufacturer's directions for using fusible web.

3. Remove the paper backing, and iron the fusible web to the wrong side of the black and white fabrics for the soccer ball and motifs as shown. Cut out each shape.

4. Peel off the paper back on each soccer ball motif. Lay out the shapes on the soccer ball appliqué. Setting the ball motifs slightly askew makes the soccer ball look realistic. Iron the soccer ball motifs in place.

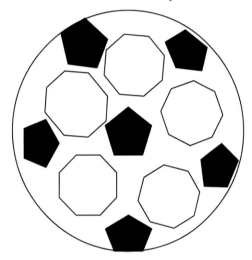

5. Remove the paper backing, and iron the soccer ball appliqué to the center of one quilted charcoal print 14½" square.

6. Sew around each appliquéd motif using a straight stitch or decorative stitch.

7. Cut the 14½" pillow front top into a 12½" square. Set aside.

8. Cut the quilted charcoal 14½" pillow back in half to measure two 7¼" x 14½" rectangles.

9. Sew the red binding strips, with right sides together, end to end. Fold in half lengthwise with wrong sides together. Press.

10. Sew the raw edge of the binding to the right side of one 14½" edge on the two 7¼" x 14½" rectangles. Turn the folded edge on the binding to the back. Hand or machine sew in place.

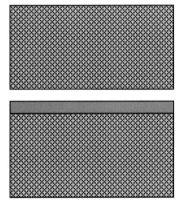

11. Place the two pillow back pieces right-side up. Overlap the two bound edges about 1½". Pin to secure. Cut into a 12½" square.

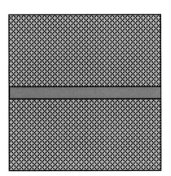

12. Place the pillow front and back with wrong sides together.

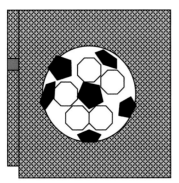

13. Pin and sew the raw edge of the red binding around the outer edge of the pillow top. Miter the corners as you sew on the binding. Overlap the ends.

14. Turn the folded edge of the binding to the back of the pillow. Hand sew in place.

15. Insert the pillow form through the envelope back.

Goal Tender
VALANCE

This fun and functional pennant valance adds a touch of victory to any bedroom a sports aficionado would love. For added appeal, make the valance in your favorite team colors.

Finished size: 20" x 40"

Preparation

1. Read all instructions before you begin.

2. Wash, dry and press all fabrics.

3. Cutting instructions are based on 40" wide fabrics. WOF = Width of Fabric.

4. Use ¼" seams throughout.

5. Press seam allowances in the direction that allows the seams to "lock" before continuing to build each block.

6. Press all seams to the dark fabric when possible.

Make the Valance

1. Turn one long edge on the 8½" x WOF black fabric strip ½" to the wrong side. Press.

2. Fold the black valance strip lengthwise with wrong sides together. Press to mark the center of the valance top. Open and place right-side up.

3. Fold the red 2½" x WOF strip lengthwise, with wrong sides together, and press.

4. Pin the raw edge of the red strip, with right sides together, on the raw long edge of the black valance top.

5. Place the black pennants with right sides together. Sew together using ¼" seams and one continuous stitched line around the pennant shapes. Trim off the point on each pennant, leaving a scant ¼" seam allowance. Turn right-side out and press.

Leave the top edge open.

Fabrics and Notions

- 1¼ yd. black print (valance)
- ⅛ yd. red print (valance trim)
- Pennant pattern from the pattern insert
- Matching thread

Tools and Supplies

- Basic sewing supplies
- Rotary cutter
- Cutting mat
- Clear ruler

Cutting Instructions

From the black print, cut:
- (1) 8½" x WOF strip
- (2) 12" x WOF strips
  From these strips, cut: (12) pennant shapes

From the red print, cut:
- (1) 2½" x WOF strip

6. Arrange and overlap the tops of the pennants on the right side of the red border. Allow a ½" excess at each end. Sew in place. Fold the red trim down. Press to make the front of the valance.

7. Fold the sides on the valance ½" to the wrong side. Sew in place to hem. Press.

8. Turn the pressed folded edge of the black fabric over the top of the pennants on the wrong side. Pin in place. Sew in place.

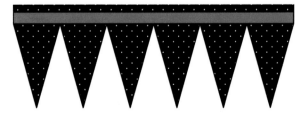

9. Sew a casing seam 1" below the top folded edge to complete the valance.

CHAPTER 4

A Hole
In One

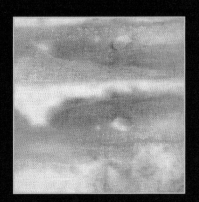

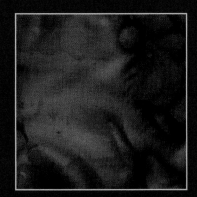

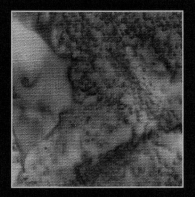

This collection is for all the golf devotees out there. Visions of making that hole in one is easy to do while bundled under this pieced quilt. The layout of the quilt has a definite formation representing the greens and bunkers on the golf course. Beautiful shades of batik fabrics enhance the overall design without the use of complicated pieced blocks. Complement the quilt by making the three coordinating pillows.

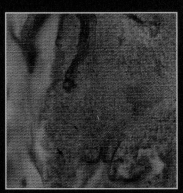

A Hole In One
QUILT

The very best golf greens cannot surpass the beauty of this quilt made with a vast variety of batik fabrics and a few simple blocks. The secret to the layout is to turn each block so that it forms a design pointing to the center panel of the quilt. Golfing dreams will come easy while sleeping under this handsome creation.

Finished size: 74" x 86"

Fabrics and Notions

- ¼ yd. tan batik No. 1 (center panel)
- ¼ yd. tan batik No. 2 (center panel)
- ¼ yd. tan batik No. 3 (center panel)
- ¼ yd. tan batik No. 4 (center panel)
- ⅔ yd. each green batik No. 1A and No. 1B (greens)
- ⅔ yd. each green batik No. 2A and No. 2B (greens)
- ⅔ yd. each green batik No. 3A and No. 3B (greens)
- ½ yd. each green batik No. 4A and No. 4B (greens)
- ½ yd. each green batik No. 5A and No. 5B (greens)
- ⅔ yd. black batik (inner border)
- 1¾ yd. dark brown or green batik (outer border, binding)
- 5 yd. backing
- Full-size batting (81" x 96")
- Matching thread

Tools and Supplies

- Basic sewing supplies
- Rotary cutter
- Cutting mat
- Clear ruler

Cutting Instructions

From each of the tan batiks, cut:
- (1) 6½" x WOF strips
  From these strips, cut: (6) 6½" squares

From the No. 1A and No. 1B green batiks, cut:
- (3) 6⅞ " x WOF strips
  From these strips, cut: (12) 6⅞" squares to equal 24 squares

From the No. 2A and No. 2B green batiks, cut
- (3) 6⅞" x WOF strips
  From these strips, cut: (12) 6⅞" squares to equal 24 squares

From the No. 3A and No. 3B green batiks, cut:
- (3) 6⅞" x WOF strips
  From these strips, cut: (12) 6⅞" squares to equal 24 squares

From the No. 4A and No. 4B green batiks, cut:
- (2) 6⅞" x WOF strips
  From these strips, cut: (6) 6⅞" squares to equal 12 squares

From the No. 5A and No. 5B green batiks, cut:
- (2) 6⅞" x WOF strips
  From these strips, cut: (6) 6⅞" squares to equal 12 squares

From the 1¾ yd. dark brown or green batik, cut:
- (9) 5½" x WOF strips (outer border)
- (9) 2½" x WOF strips (binding)

From the black batik, cut:
- (8) 2" x WOF strips (inner border)

Preparation

1. Read all instructions before you begin.

2. Wash, dry and press all fabrics.

3. Cutting instructions are based on 40" wide fabrics. WOF = Width of Fabric.

4. Use ¼" seams throughout.

5. Press seam allowances in the direction that allows the seams to "lock" before continuing to build each block.

6. Press all seams to the dark fabric when possible.

Build the Blocks

Make (96) 6½" Half-Square Triangle Blocks

1. Keep all like fabrics together at all times.

2. Sort colors, keeping like colors together. Label each group of squares (No. 1A, No. 1B, etc.)

Green No. 1 (A)	Green No. 2 (A)	Green No. 3 (A)	Green No. 4 (A)	Green No. 5 (A)
Green No. 1 (B)	Green No. 2 (B)	Green No. 3 (B)	Green No. 4 (B)	Green No. 5 (B)

3. Draw a diagonal line across the wrong side on the No. 1A green batik 6⅞" squares.

4. Place the drawn-on No. 1A green batik squares, with right sides together, on the No. 1B green batik 6⅞" squares.

5. Sew a ¼" seam on each side of the drawn line.

6. Cut apart on the drawn line.

7. Open and press. Yield: 24 green batik 1A/1B blocks. Set aside.

8. Repeat Steps 2 through 7 with No. 2A and No. 2B green batik 6⅞" squares. Yield: 24 green batik 2A/2B blocks.

9. Repeat Steps 2 through 7 with No. 3A and No. 3B green batik 6⅞" squares. Yield: 24 green batik 3A/3B blocks.

10. Repeat Steps 2 through 7 with No. 4A and No. 4B green batik 6⅞" squares. Yield: 12 green batik 4A/4B blocks.

11. Repeat Steps 2 through 7 with No. 5A and No. 5B green batik 6⅞" squares. Yield: 12 green batik 5A/5B blocks.

Build the Center Panel

Refer to the quilt layout on page 57 often.

1. Sort and label all tan fabrics.

Tan No. 1 Cut six	Tan No. 2 Cut six	Tan No. 3 Cut six	Tan No. 4 Cut six

2. Lay out the center panel as shown.

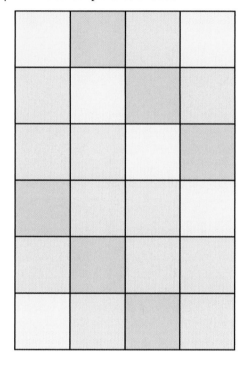

3. With right sides together, sew four blocks together for each row. Press. Set each row aside on a flat surface, keeping the rows in order.

4. With right sides together, sew the six rows together. Press. Set aside.

Build the Quilt

Refer to the quilt photo and layout often.

The quilt is constructed of four sections that are sewn to the center panel.

The side sections mirror each other to form the design pattern. The blocks on the top and bottom sections on the quilt also are divided at the center. When laying out and sewing the blocks together, it is important to remember that each side of the top and bottom sections mirror the other side to achieve the design pattern. (Some blocks need to be turned to form the design pattern.)

Keep all like fabrics of the half-square triangle blocks together until they are laid out to form each section of the quilt as shown.

Section 1

1. Sew the five blocks, with right sides together, to make the row.

2. Sew the three rows of blocks together with right sides together. Press and set aside.

Row 1	1AB	2AB	3AB	4AB	5AB
Row 2					
Row 3					

Section 2

1. Sew the five blocks, with right sides together, to make the row.

2. Sew the three rows of blocks together with right sides together. Press and set aside.

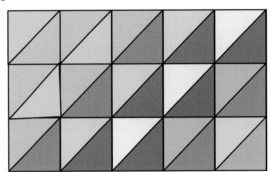

helpful hint

Pin a small scrap of paper with the name of each block on each block as shown. This will help keep the half-square triangle blocks together without turning or misplacing them.

Rows also can be labeled as shown. Sew the blocks together that are numbered together. Remove the numbered papers. Repeat for the next row.

1 AB	2 AB	3 AB	4 AB	5 AB

Row No. 1	Row No. 2	Row No. 3

Section 3

1. Sew the six blocks, with right sides together, to make the row.

2. With right sides together, sew the three rows together. Press and set aside.

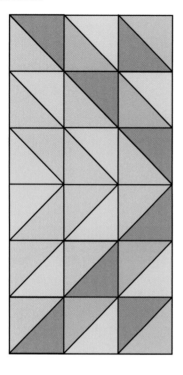

Section 4

1. Sew the six blocks, with right sides together, to make the row.

2. With right sides together, sew the three rows together. Press and set aside.

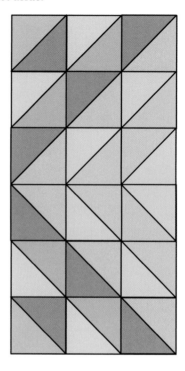

Section 5

1. Sew the five blocks, with right sides together, to make the row.

2. With right sides together, sew the three rows together. Press and set aside.

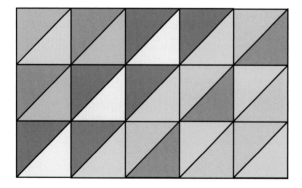

Section 6

1. Sew the five blocks, with right sides together, to make the row.

2. With right sides together sew the three rows together. Press and set aside.

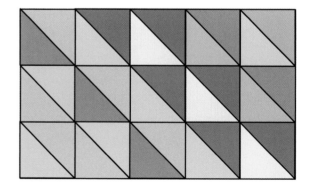

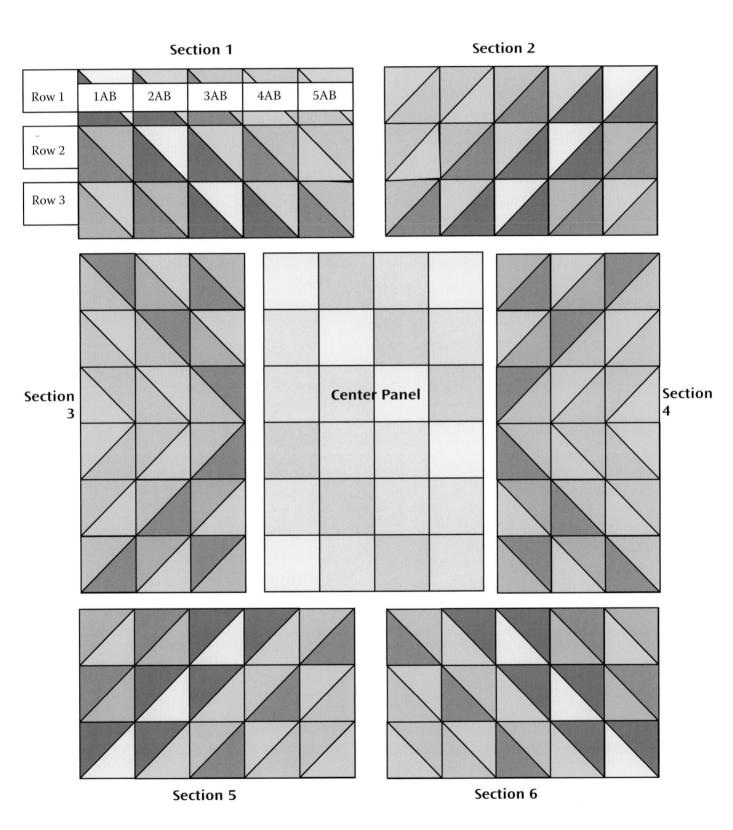

Section 1

Row 1	1AB	2AB	3AB	4AB	5AB
Row 2					
Row 3					

Section 2

Section 3

Section 4

Center Panel

Section 5

Section 6

Build the Quilt Center

1. With right sides together, sew Section 1 and Section 2 together to make the quilt top. Press. Repeat with Sections 5 and 6 to make the quilt bottom.

2. Sew side Sections 3 and 4, with right sides together, to the center panel. Press.

3. With right sides together, sew the top and bottom sections to the quilt. Press.

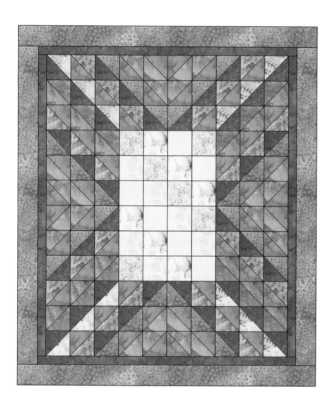

Finish the Quilt

Refer to the General Instructions for detailed instructions on binding and borders on page 13.

1. Sew the 2½" x WOF black inner border strips, with right sides together, end to end.

2. Measure all the sides of the quilt. Cut each inner border strip to fit the top, bottom and sides of the quilt center.

3. With right sides together, sew the side inner borders to the quilt center. Press. With right sides together, sew the top and bottom inner borders to the quilt.

4. Sew the green 5½" x WOF border strips, with right sides together, end to end.

5. Measure the quilt again and cut the green side, top and bottom outer border strips.

6. With right sides together, sew the green border strips to the sides. With right sides together, sew the green top and bottom borders to the quilt. Press.

7. Layer the backing (face down), batting and quilt top (face up). Baste and quilt as desired. The model was quilted using an overall meander design.

8. Sew the binding strips, with right sides together, end to end.

9. Fold the binding strips in half lengthwise, with wrong sides together, and press.

10. Sew the raw edge of the binding to the outer edge of the quilt top, mitering the corners as you sew.

11. Trim the batting and backing fabric, leaving ¼" seam allowance around the edge of the quilt.

12. Turn the folded edge of the binding to the back of the quilt. Hand sew in place.

Golf Square
PILLOW

This soft, pieced pillow shows the half-square triangle blocks as displayed in the quilt. The simple pillow design is bordered with the black batik fabric and the multi-faceted cream batik border. Fill the pillow with a pillow form or soft poly fill.

Finished size: 18" square

Preparation

1. Read all instructions before you begin.

2. Wash, dry and press all fabrics.

3. Cutting instructions are based on 40" wide fabrics. WOF = Width of Fabric.

4. Use ¼" seams throughout.

5. Press seam allowances in the direction that allows the seams to "lock" before continuing to build each block.

6. Press all seams to the dark fabric when possible.

Make the Golf Square Pillow

1. Draw a diagonal line across the wrong side of the 6⅞" cream squares.

2. Place the drawn-on squares, right sides together, on the 6⅞" green squares.

3. Sew a ¼" seam on each side of the drawn line.

4. Trim, leaving a ¼" seam allowance. Open and press.

 5. Sew two half-square triangle blocks together. Repeat with two more blocks. Press.

 6. Sew the two sets together to make the pillow center panel. Press.

7. Measure the sides of the pillow center and cut the 1½" black border strips to match. With right sides together, sew on the side border strips. Repeat for the top and bottom borders. Press.

8. Measure the sides of the pillow and cut the 2½" cream border strips to match. Sew the cream borders to the sides. Repeat for the top and bottom borders.

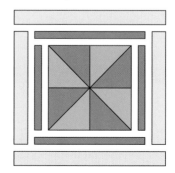

Fabrics and Notions

- Fat quarter green batik (half-square triangle blocks)
- ⅔ yd. cream batik (half-square triangle blocks, border, back)
- ⅓ yd. black batik (inner border, binding)
- ⅔ yd. muslin (quilting foundation)
- ⅔ yd. batting (quilting foundation)
- Pillow form or poly fill
- Matching thread

Tools and Supplies

- Basic sewing supplies
- Rotary cutter
- Cutting mat
- Clear ruler

Cutting Instructions

From the green batik, cut:
- (2) 6⅞" squares

From the cream batik, cut:
- (2) 6⅞" squares
- (2) 2½" x WOF strips
- (1) 20" square

From the black batik, cut:
- (1) 1½" x WOF strip (inner border)
- (2) 2½" x WOF strip (binding)

From the muslin, cut:
- (2) 22" Squares

From the batting, cut:
- (2) 22" squares

Finish the Pillow

Refer to the General Instructions for making pillows on pages 12 and 13.

1. Layer the muslin, batting and pillow back (face up). Repeat for the pillow front.

2. Baste and quilt as desired. The model was quilted using an overall, meander quilting technique.

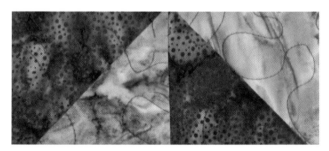

3. Trim the batting and muslin to ¼" around all the edges on the pillow top and back.

4. Match the pillow top and back with wrong sides together. Baste or pin the layers together.

5. Sew the black binding strips, with right sides together, end to end. Fold in half lengthwise with wrong sides together. Press.

6. Sew the raw edge of the binding to the outer edge of the pillow top. Miter the corners as the binding is sewn on. Leave a 10" opening. Pin the binding to the top fabric edge on the opening.

7. Insert the stuffing or pillow form. Sew the pinned binding in place to connect the pillow front and back.

8. Turn the folded edge of the binding to the back of the pillow. Hand sew in place.

Golf Bag Appliqué
PILLOW

The golf bag silhouette on this pillow adds a touch of class. The decorative and easy, iron-on appliqué is outline stitched and quilted using a small, meander quilting technique. This pillow would make a great gift for your favorite golf pro.

Finished size: 12" x 21"

Make the Pillow

1. Cut the 1½" black border strips for the sides of the 6½" x 15½" cream pillow center. With right sides together, sew in place. Repeat for the top and bottom borders.

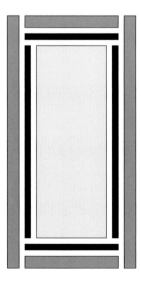

2. Measure the pillow top sides and cut the 2½" green border strips to match. With right sides together, sew the green borders to the sides of the pillow. Repeat for the top and bottom borders.

3. Trace around the golf bag pattern on the sticky side of the iron-on fusible web paper. Cut out the shape allowing ½" excess around the shape. Follow the manufacturer's directions for fusible web.

4. Peel off the paper back on the golf bag appliqué. Iron the appliqué to the wrong side of the black batik fabric. Cut out on the drawn line.

Preparation

1. Read all instructions before you begin.

2. Wash, dry and press all fabrics.

3. Cutting instructions are based on 40" wide fabrics. WOF = Width of Fabric.

4. Use ¼" seams throughout.

5. Press seam allowances in the direction that allows the seams to "lock" before continuing to build each block.

6. Press all seams to the dark fabric when possible.

Fabrics and Notions

- ½ yd. cream batik (center panel)
- ½ yd. green batik (border, backing)
- ½ yd. black batik (inner border, binding)
- Golf bag pattern from pattern insert
- ½ yd. muslin
- ½ yd. batting
- ½ yd. iron-on fusible web
- Matching thread

Tools and Supplies

- Basic sewing supplies
- Rotary cutter
- Cutting mat
- Clear ruler

Cutting Instructions

From the cream batik, cut:
- (1) 6½" x 15½" rectangle

From the green batik, cut:
- (2) 1½" x WOF strips
- (1) 18" x 24" backing

From the black batik, cut:
- (2) 1½" x WOF strips (inner border)
- (2) 2½" x WOF strips (binding)
- (1) "fused golf bag"

Note: See the directions for fusing the fabric.

---

5. Peel off the remaining paper on the golf bag appliqué. Arrange the golf bag appliqué on the pillow center.

6. Iron the appliqué in place on the pillow front panel.

7. Sew around the appliqué using a straight stitch or decorative stitch.

8. Layer the muslin, batting and pillow top (face up). Repeat for the pillow back.

9. Pin or baste and quilt as desired. A small, meander quilting technique was used on the model.

Finish the Pillow

Refer to the General Instructions for making pillows on pages 12 and 13.

1. Place the quilted front and back of the pillow with wrong sides together. Pin to secure.

2. Sew the binding strips, with right sides together, end to end. Fold in half lengthwise with wrong sides together. Press.

3. Pin and sew the raw edge of the binding to the outer edge of the pillow top. Miter the corners as you attach the binding. Leave a 10" opening at the bottom to stuff the pillow.

4. Pin the binding in place to the top opening of fabric.

5. Stuff the pillow firmly.

6. Sew the opening and binding in place.

7. Turn the folded edge of the binding to the back of the pillow. Hand sew in place.

Hole In One Golf

PILLOW

This toss pillow is made with six half-square triangle blocks. Use a variety of rich-looking batiks to match your masculine décor. The borders and binding grace the center panel on this handsome pillow.

Finished size: 18" x 24"

Preparation

1. Read all instructions before you begin.

2. Wash, dry and press all fabrics.

3. Cutting instructions are based on 40" wide fabrics. WOF = Width of Fabric.

4. Use ¼" seams throughout.

5. Press seam allowances in the direction that allows the seams to "lock" before continuing to build each block.

6. Press all seams to the dark fabric when possible.

Make the Half-Square Triangle Blocks
Make six 6½" blocks

1. Draw a diagonal line across the wrong side of the cream 6⅞" squares.

2. Place the drawn-on squares, with right sides together, on the 6⅞" green squares.

3. Sew a ¼" seam on each side of the drawn line.

4. Cut apart on the drawn line. Open and press.

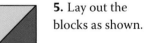

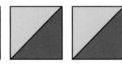

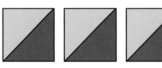

5. Lay out the blocks as shown.

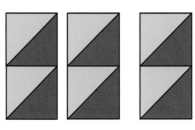

6. With right sides together, sew the half-square triangle blocks together in pairs. Press.

Fabrics and Notions

- ¼ yd. green batik (blocks)
- 1 yd. cream batik (blocks, outer border, backing)
- ⅓ yd. black batik (inner border, binding)
- ¾ yd. muslin (quilting foundation)
- ¾ yd. batting (quilting foundation)
- Matching thread
- Poly fill

Tools and Supplies

- Basic sewing supplies
- Rotary cutter
- Cutting mat
- Clear ruler

Cutting Instructions

From the green batik, cut:
- (3) 6⅞" squares

From the cream batik, cut:
- (3) 6⅞" squares
- (2) 2½" x WOF strips
  From these strips, cut: (2) 18½" strips and (2) 20½" strips
- (1) 22" x 28" backing

From the black batik, cut:
- (2) 1½" x WOF strips
- (3) 2½" x WOF strips

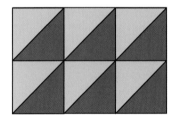

7. Sew the pairs of blocks, with right sides together, to make the center of the pillow. Press.

8. Measure the sides of the pillow center. Cut the 1½" black border strips to match. Sew the side border strips, with right sides together, to the pillow. Repeat for the top and bottom borders. Press.

9. Repeat Step 8 to add the cream 2½" border strips.

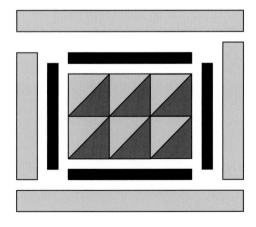

Finish the Pillow

Refer to the General Instructions for making pillows on pages 12 and 13.

1. Layer the muslin, batting and pillow top (face up). Repeat for the pillow back.

2. Baste or pin and quilt as desired. A medium, meander quilting technique was used on the model.

3. Pin the quilted pillow front and back with wrong sides together.

4. Sew the black 2½" binding strips, with right sides together, end to end. Fold in half lengthwise with wrong sides together. Press.

5. Pin and sew the raw edge of the binding to the outer edge of the pillow top. Miter the corners as the binding is attached. Leave a 10" opening for stuffing the pillow. Pin the binding to the top fabric edge across the opening.

6. Stuff the pillow firmly. Continue to sew the binding in place, connecting the pillow front and back.

7. Turn the folded edge of the binding to the back of the pillow. Hand sew in place.

CHAPTER 5

Geese On The Run

This rugged collection of a rag-seam quilt, chenille pillow and a rag rug has a hearty feel and is fun to create. The blocks of the quilt are pre-quilted before they are sewn. The seams are sewn together allowing the raw edge of the fabrics to come forward before they are clipped. Machine washing and drying the quilt lets each clipped seam fray, adding even more character. The rug and pillow are made using the chenille technique of quilting. Enjoy the quick process of sewing the top, batting and backing together and quilting the pieces as you go. Easy-pieced borders finish these robust and manly projects.

Geese on the Run
QUILT

This raggy quilt is great fun to make as well as use. Bundle up next to the fireplace or campfire in this cuddly, homespun flannel creation. It makes a comfy take-along blanket for those chilly evenings under the stars or a quiet evening at home. The piecing and rag seam techniques give the quilt an interesting appeal. What man, young or old, wouldn't be pleased to receive a gift like this!

Finished size: 63" x 81"

Fabrics and Notions

- 3 yd. red plaid homespun (rectangle front and back blocks)
- 3 yd. green check homespun (rectangle front and back blocks)
- 2½ yd. gold plaid homespun (flying geese squares)
- 5⅓ yd. black plaid homespun (flying geese rectangles, backing strips, binding)
- Full-size batting (81" x 96")
- Matching thread

Tools and Supplies

- Basic sewing supplies
- Rotary cutter
- Cutting mat
- Clear ruler

Cutting Instructions

From the red plaid homespun, cut:
- (18) 5½" x WOF strips
  From these strips, cut: (72) 5½" x 10" rectangles

From the green check homespun, cut:
- (18) 5½" x WOF strips
  From these strips, cut: (72) 5½" x 10" rectangles

From the black plaid homespun, cut:
- (18) 5½" x WOF strips
  From these strips, cut: (54) 5½" x 10½" rectangles
- (6) 10½" x WOF strips (backing strips)
- (8) 2½" x WOF (binding strips)

From the gold plaid homespun, cut:
- (16) 5½" x WOF strips
  From these strips, cut: (108) 5½" squares

From the batting, cut:
- (3) 9" x 84" strips (flying geese units)
- (72) 4½" x 9" rectangles (blocks)

Preparation

1. Read all instructions before you begin.

2. Wash, dry and press all fabrics.

3. Cutting instructions are based on 40" wide fabrics. WOF = Width of Fabric.

4. Use ¼" seams throughout.

5. Press seam allowances in the direction that allows the seams to "lock" before continuing to build each block.

6. Press all seams to the dark fabric when possible.

Build the Blocks

Make (72) 5½" x 10" rectangle blocks.

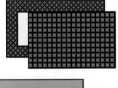

1. Sandwich the 4½" x 9" batting rectangles between two 5½" x 10" red plaid rectangles. Pin together to secure. Repeat with the 5½" x 10" green check rectangles.

2. Meander quilt each rectangle to within ½" from the edge. Make 36 red and 36 green 5½" x 10" rectangle blocks. Set aside.

Make (54) 5" x 10" Flying Geese blocks

The Flying Geese blocks will be trimmed to 5" x 10".

1. Draw a diagonal line across the wrong side on the gold plaid 5½" squares.

2. Place a 5½" drawn-on gold plaid square, with right sides together, on the **right** side of the 5½" x 10½" black plaid rectangle.

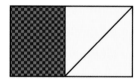

3. Sew on the drawn line. Trim, leaving a ¼" seam. Open and press.

4. Repeat Step 2 on the **left** side of each 5½" x 10½" black plaid rectangle.

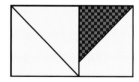

5. Trim the top or pointed edge on each block leaving ¼" seam.

6. Trim the block sides to make 5" x 10" blocks.

7. With right sides together, place a pin at each point.

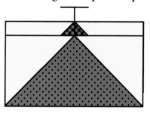

8. Sew the flying geese blocks, with right sides together, into three vertical rows of 18 blocks.

9. With right sides together, sew two of the 10" x WOF black plaid homespun strips together end to end. Repeat to make three sets of backing strips for the flying geese rows.

10. Layer the 9" x 84" batting strips between the backing fabric (face down) and the flying geese rows. Pin to secure. Repeat on the remaining two sets.

11. Quilt each section as desired. The model was meander quilted.

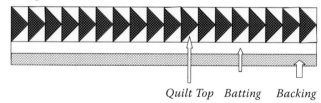

Quilt Top   Batting   Backing

helpful hint

"UP" Seams

Rag quilt seams are sewn with wrong sides together and ½" seams. This allows the seam to show on the right side of the project, creating the rag look.

Build the Quilt

Refer to the quilt layout.

1. Sew the red plaid rectangles to the green check rectangles with wrong sides together, sewing the seams ½" "UP."

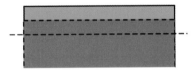

2. Sew the blocks together to make four rows of 18 rectangles.

3. Sew the rectangle rows to the flying geese rows, sewing the seams ½" "UP".

Finish the Quilt

Refer to the General Instructions for mitering bindings on page 13.

1. Sew the binding strips, with right sides together, end to end. Fold in half lengthwise, with wrong sides together, and press. Sew the raw edge on the binding to the outer edge on the quilt, mitering the corners as the binding is attached.

2. Turn the folded edge of the binding to the back. Hand sew in place.

3. Clip all "UP" seams to the sewn line every ¼".

4. Wash and dry the quilt. Remove all lint from the washer and dryer. Shake the quilt outside to remove the excess threads. Sticky tape will remove any additional threads.

RUG
Geese On The Run

Soft and durable, this rug adds a very creative accent to the Geese on the Run collection. The center of the rug is made using the chenille quilting technique, while the borders are pieced, Flying Geese blocks. The rug grip product can be sewn to the rug to keep it from slipping on slick surfaces. Create one for every room in the house!

Finished size: 24" x 33"

Fabrics and Notions

- 2 yd. black plaid homespun (center, flying geese blocks, backing, binding)
- 1 yd. gold plaid homespun (center, flying geese blocks)
- ¾ yd. green check homespun (center)
- ¾ yd. red plaid homespun (center)
- 1½ yd. batting
- Matching thread

Tools and Supplies

- Basic sewing supplies
- Rotary cutter
- Cutting mat
- Clear ruler
- Scissors or slash cutter
- Water erasable pen
- Rug backing 24" x 33"

Cutting Instructions

From the black plaid homespun, cut:
- (1) 24½" center square
- (2) 4½" x WOF strips
  From these strips, cut: (6) 4½" x 8½" rectangles
- (1) 27" x 40" rectangle (backing)
- (3) 2½" x WOF strips (binding)

From the gold print, cut:
- (1) 24½" center square
- (2) 4½" x WOF strips
  From these strips, cut: (12) 4½" squares

From the green check homespun, cut:
- (1) 24½" center square

From the red plaid homespun, cut:
- (1) 24½" center square

From the batting, cut:
- (2) 27" x 45" rectangles

Preparation

1. Read all instructions before you begin.

2. Wash, dry and press all fabrics.

3. Cutting instructions are based on 40" wide fabrics. WOF = Width of Fabric.

4. Use ¼" seams throughout.

5. Press seam allowances in the direction that allows the seams to "lock" before continuing to build each block.

6. Press all seams to the dark fabric when possible.

Build the Rug

1. Layer the two pieces of batting on top of the black plaid backing fabric.

2. Layer and center the four 24½" black, gold, green and red fabrics. Pin in place to secure.

3. Sew diagonal seams every ½" through all layers. Follow the plaid lines or draw diagonal lines every ½" using a water-erasable pen. Set aside.

4. Carefully insert the scissors between the back fabric and the three top layers. Cut the three top layers between each sewn diagonal line.

Make the Flying Geese Blocks

1. Draw a diagonal line across the wrong side on the 4½" gold plaid squares.

2. Place the drawn-on squares, with right sides together, on the **right** side of the 4½" x 8½" black plaid rectangles.

3. Sew on the drawn line. Do not trim. Open and press. Repeat on the **left** side on the rectangle.

4. Make six Flying Geese blocks.

5. Refer to the photo. Sew together three Flying Geese blocks with right sides together. Repeat.

6. Pin the Flying Geese block units, with right sides together, on the 24½" ends of the rug. Sew in place using ¼" seams. Open and press.

7. Stitch in the ditch to quilt the Flying Geese blocks.

Finish the Rug

Refer to the General Instructions for mitering bindings on page 13.

1. Sew the 2½" binding strips, with right sides together, end to end.

2. Fold the binding in half lengthwise with wrong sides together. Press.

3. Sew the raw edge of the binding to the outer edge on the rug top. Miter the corners as the binding is attached.

4. Trim the backing fabric and batting, leaving ¼" seam allowance around the edge of the rug.

5. Turn the folded edge of the rug to the back. Hand sew in place.

6. Wash and dry the rug. Shake the rug to remove any excess threads. Remove any lint from the washer and dryer.

PILLOW

Toss this large throw pillow on the couch or floor and cuddle under the matching quilt to watch your favorite movie or read your favorite book. The chenille front panel on the pillow makes the pillow "squeezably" soft. Sew several as gifts for friends, family members and yourself!

Finished size: 24" square

Fabrics and Notions

- ¾ yd. black plaid homespun (pillow center, flying geese)
- 1¾ yd. gold plaid homespun (backing, flying geese)
- ½ yd. green check homespun (center)
- ¾ yd. red plaid homespun (center, binding)
- Polyester stuffing or 24" pillow form
- Matching thread

Tools and Supplies

- Basic sewing supples
- Rotary cutter
- Cutting mat
- Clear ruler

Cutting Instructions

From the black plaid homespun, cut:
- (1) 16½" square
- (3) 4½" x WOF for strips
  From these strips, cut: (4) 4½" squares
  and (8) 4½" x 8½" rectangles

From the gold plaid homespun, cut:
- (1) 16½" square
- (1) 30" square
- (2) 4½" x WOF strips
  From these strips, cut: (16) 4½" squares

From the green check homespun, cut:
- (1) 16½" square

From the red plaid, cut:
- (1) 16½" square
- (3) 2½" x WOF strips

Preparation

1. Read all instructions before you begin.

2. Wash, dry and press all fabrics.

3. Cutting instructions are based on 40" wide fabrics. WOF = Width of Fabric.

4. Use ¼" seams throughout.

5. Press seam allowances in the direction that allows the seams to "lock" before continuing to build each block.

6. Press all seams to the dark fabric when possible.

Build the Pillow

Make eight 4½" x 8½" Flying Geese blocks.

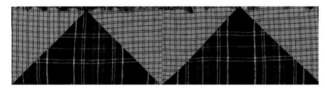

1. Draw diagonal lines across the wrong side on each 4½" gold plaid square.

2. Place the drawn-on squares, with right sides together, on the **right** side of each 4½" x 8½" black plaid rectangle. Sew on the drawn line. Trim, open and press. Repeat on the **left** side of each rectangle.

Make eight.

Make the Center Panel

1. Layer the 16½" black plaid, gold plaid and green check on top of the 16½" red plaid square.

2. Draw diagonal lines every ½" across the top 16½".

3. Sew on the drawn lines or follow the plaid lines, sewing diagonal seams every ½" across the complete top square, connecting all fabric layers.

4. Carefully insert the scissors and cut through the three top layers of fabric between the seam lines. Set aside.

Add the Borders

1. Sew four sets of two Flying Geese blocks with right sides together. Press.

2. Sew a black plaid 4½" square to the ends of two sets of the Flying Geese blocks. Open and press.

3. Sew the side flying geese borders (the ones without the black squares) to the pillow center with right sides together. Sew the top and bottom borders, with right sides together, to the pillow top.

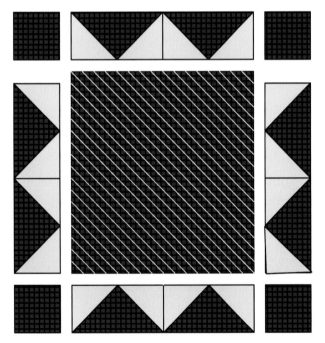

Finish the Pillow

Refer to the General Instructions for mitering bindings on page 13.

1. Cut the 30" backing fabric in half. Fold the center edges under until the backing fabric fits across the pillow top, overlapping the center about 2". Trim all sides to fit.

2. Pin the pillow top and backing pieces with wrong sides together.

3. Sew the binding strips, with right sides together, end to end. Fold in half lengthwise with wrong sides together. Press.

4. Sew the raw edge of the binding around the outer edge of the pillow top. Miter the corners as the binding is attached.

5. Trim the fabric, leaving a ¼" seam allowance around the edge of the pillow.

6. Turn the folded edge of the binding to the back. Hand sew in place.

7. Insert stuffing or pillow form through the envelope back.

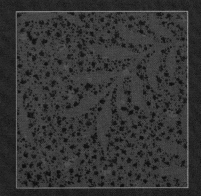

CHAPTER 6

The Western Way

The open range, prairie, star-filled skies and the spirited cowboy all portray the American West. What better way to recognize the hard-working men in your life, than with this captivating collection of small and large quilts.

The easy-pieced boot and star blocks are made with rich-leather, blue-star and red cotton-print fabrics.

Create this collection as a welcome invitation for friends and family.

The Western Way
QUILT

Dream of wide-open spaces and rolling plains when sleeping under this quilt. The boots and stars will brighten any bedroom or bunkhouse. The blocks are easy to make and simply call up the tradition of the wonderful western lifestyle. Let the "cowboy" in your life sleep in comfort and style.

Finished size: 82" x 96"

Fabrics and Notions

- 1½ yd. cream print (background)
- 3 yd. brown leather-print (boot top, cornerstones, outer border)
- ⅔ yd. brown texture-print (boot bottom)
- 1/8 yd. black print (boot heel)
- 2¼ yd. dark blue print (background)
- 1¼ yd. gold print (star points)
- ⅔ yd. red-gold print (small star center square)
- 1½ yd. red print (sashing, inner border)
- 7 yd. for backing
- Queen-size batting (90" x 108")
- Matching thread

Tools and Supplies

- Basic sewing supplies
- Rotary cutter
- Cutting mat
- Clear ruler

Cutting Instructions for the Double Star Block

From the dark blue print, cut:
- (16) 3½" x WOF strips
  From these strips, cut: (60) 3½" squares and (60) 3½" x 6½" rectangles
- (9) 2" x WOF strips
  From these strips, cut: (60) 2" squares and (60) 2½" x 3½" rectangles

From the gold print, cut:
- (11) 3½" x WOF strips
  From these strips, cut: (120) 3½" squares

From the red-gold print, cut
- (2) 3½" x WOF strips
  From these strips, cut: (15) 3½" squares
- (7) 2" x WOF strips
  From these strips, cut: (120) 2" squares

Cutting Instructions for Boot Block

From the cream print, cut:
- (1) 12½" x WOF strip
  From this strip, cut: (15) 2½" x 12½" rectangles
- (2) 10½" x WOF strips
  From these strips, cut: (15) 4½" x 10½" rectangles
- (3) 1½" x WOF strips
  From these strips, cut: (15) 1½" x 6½" rectangles
- (2) 2" x WOF strips
  From these strips, cut: (30) 2" squares.
- (2) 1½" x WOF strips
  From these strips, cut: (30) 1½" squares

From the brown leather-print, cut:
- (9) 5½" x WOF strips (outer border)
- (9) 2½" x WOF strips (binding)
- (3) 7½" x WOF strips
  From these strips, cut: (15) 6½" x 7½" rectangles
- (2) 2" x WOF strips
  From these strips, cut: (20) 2" squares

From the brown texture-print, cut:
- (1) 6½" x WOF strip
  From this strip, cut: (15) 2½" x 6½" rectangles
- (1) 2½" x WOF strips
  From this strip, cut: (15) 2½" squares
- (1) 7½" x WOF strips
  From this strip, cut: (15) 2½" x 7½" rectangles

From the black print cut:
- (1) 3½" x WOF strips
  From this strip, cut: (15) 2½" x 3½" rectangles

Cutting Instructions for the Sashing and Inner Border

From the red print, cut:
- (17) 2" x WOF strips
  From these strips, cut: (49) 2" x 12½" rectangles
- (8) 2" x WOF strips

From the brown leather-print, cut:
- (9) 5½" x WOF strips
- (9) 2½" x WOF strips
- (3) 7½" x WOF strips
  From these strips, cut: (15) 6½" x 7½" rectangles
- (2) 2" x WOF strips
  From these strips, cut: (20) 2" squares

Preparation

1. Read all instructions before you begin.

2. Wash, dry and press all fabrics.

3. Cutting instructions are based on 40" wide fabrics. WOF = Width of Fabric.

4. Use ¼" seams throughout.

5. Press seam allowances in the direction that allows the seams to "lock" before continuing to build each block.

6. Press all seams to the dark fabric when possible.

Build the Boot Blocks

Make (15) 12½" blocks.

Refer to the block layout often.

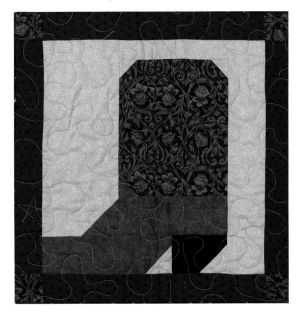

1. Draw a diagonal line on the wrong side of the cream 1½" and 2" squares.

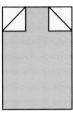

2. Place the drawn-on 1½" cream squares, with right sides together, on the top corners on one 6½" x 7½" brown leather-print rectangle. Sew on the drawn line. Trim, leaving a ¼" seam allowance. Open and press.

3. Draw a diagonal line across the wrong side on the 2½" brown texture-print squares.

4. Place the drawn-on square, right sides together, on the lower right corner on the 4½" x 10½" cream rectangle. Sew on the drawn line. Trim, leaving a ¼" seam allowance. Open and press.

5. Place a drawn-on 2" cream square, with right sides together, on the lower right corner of the 2½" x 7½" brown texture-print rectangle. Sew on the drawn line. Trim, leaving a ¼" seam allowance. Open and press.

6. Place the remaining drawn-on 2" cream square, with right sides together, on the lower right corner on the 2½" x 3½" black print rectangle. Sew on the drawn line. Trim, leaving a ¼" seam allowance. Open and press.

7. Refer to the block layout.

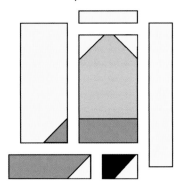

8. Lay out the block. Sew the block together from the top to the bottom.

9. Sew the 1½" x 6½" cream rectangle, with right sides together, to the top of the 6½" x 7½" brown leather-print rectangle. Press.

10. Sew the 2½" x 6½" brown texture-print, with right sides together, to the bottom of the 6½" x 7½" brown leather-print rectangle. Press.

11. With right sides together, sew the 4½" x 10½" cream rectangle to the left side of the boot top.

12. With right sides together, sew the boot heel and boot toe sections together. Press.

13. Sew the boot bottom, with right sides together, to the boot top. Press.

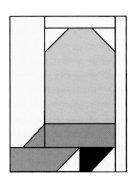

14. Sew the 2½" x 12½" cream background rectangle to the right side of the boot block. Press.

15. Repeat to make a total of 15 blocks 12½" square.

Build the Double Star Blocks
Make (15) 12½" blocks

1. Draw diagonal lines on the wrong side of the 3½" gold squares and the 2" red-gold squares.

2. Place a 3½" drawn-on gold square, with right sides together, on the **right** side of the dark blue 3½" x 6½" rectangles. Sew on the drawn line. Trim, leaving a ¼" seam allowance. Open and press.

3. Repeat, and sew the 3½" gold squares, with right sides together, on the **left** side of each 3½" x 6½" dark blue rectangle. Set aside.

4. Place a drawn-on 2" red-gold square, with right sides together, on the **right** side of the 2" x 3½" dark blue rectangle. Sew on the drawn line. Trim, leaving a ¼" seam allowance. Open and press.

5. Repeat Step 1 through Step 4 on the **left** side of each rectangle to make 60 star point units. Press. Lay out each block as shown on the diagram.

6. Sew a 2" dark blue corner square, with right sides together, to the ends of the top and bottom star point units. Sew the remaining star point units to the sides of the 3½" dark blue center squares. Open and press.

7. Sew the top and bottom star point units, with right sides together, to the center square. Press.

8. Sew the gold star point units, with right sides together, to the sides of the center star.

9. Sew a 3½" dark blue square, with right sides together, to the ends of the top and bottom star point units. Press.

10. Sew the top and bottom star point units, with right sides together, onto the center star. Press.

Build the Quilt

Lay out the quilt as shown.

1. Sew a 2" x 12½" red sashing rectangle, with right sides together, to the right side of the first four blocks in each row.

2. With right sides together, sew a 2" brown leather-print corner square to the right side of four 2" x 12½" sashing rectangles. Sew the four sets together.

3. Finish by sewing a sashing to the right side. Repeat to make five rows of sashing.

4. Sew the rows of blocks, with right sides together, to the sashing rows making the center of the quilt.

5. Sew the 2" red inner border strips, with right sides together, end to end.

6. Measure the sides of the quilt. Cut the border strips to match. Sew the side border strips, with right sides together, to the quilt. Repeat for the top and bottom borders.

7. Sew the nine 5½" brown leather-print border strips, with right sides together, end to end.

8. Measure the sides of the quilt. Cut the border strips to match. Sew the side border strips, with right sides together, to the quilt. Repeat for the top and bottom borders. Press.

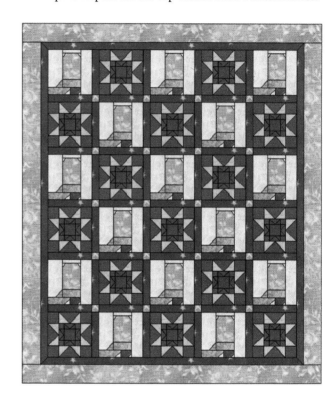

Finish the Quilt

Refer to the General Instructions for mitering bindings on page 13.

1. Layer the backing (face down), batting, and quilt top (face up). Baste and quilt as desired. The model was quilted using a free-form, meander technique with loops and stars.

2. Sew the 2½" brown leather-print binding strips, with right sides together, end to end. Fold in half lengthwise with wrong sides together. Press.

3. Sew the raw edge of the binding to the outer edge of the quilt top. Miter the corners as you attach the binding.

4. Trim the batting and backing fabric, leaving a ¼" seam allowance around the edge of the quilt.

5. Turn the folded edge of the binding to the back. Hand sew in place.

WALL QUILT

The Western Way

Add this fun wall quilt to your western-themed bedroom or den and let the decorating begin. Horseshoes, barbwire plaques and other western gear are just a few ideas to complete the setting.

Finished size: 16" x 30"

Fabrics and Notions

- Fat quarter cream print (background)
- ⅔ yd. brown leather-print (boot top, border, binding)
- ⅛ yd. brown texture-print (boot bottom)
- ⅛ yd. black print (boot heel)
- ⅛ yd. red print (cornerstone squares)
- ¼ yd. dark blue print (background)
- ⅔ yd. gold print (sashing, backing)
- ⅔ yd. batting
- 3 "O" ½" rings
- Matching thread

Tools and Supplies

- Basic sewing supplies
- Rotary cutter
- Cutting mat
- Clear ruler

Cutting Instructions

From the cream print, cut:
- (1) 1½" x 7½" rectangle
- (1) 4½" x 12½" rectangle
- (1) 1½" x 14½" rectangle
- (2) 2½" squares
- (2) 2" squares

From the brown leather-print, cut:
- (1) 7½" x 9½" rectangle
- (2) 2½" x 26½" border strips
- (2) 2½" x 16½" border strips

From the brown texture-print, cut:
- (1) 2½" x 8½" rectangle
- (1) 2½" x 7½" rectangle
- (1) 2½" square

From the black print, cut:
- (1) 2½" x 3½" rectangle

From the gold print, cut:
- (2) 1½" x WOF strips
  From these strips, cut: (16) 1½" x 2½" rectangles and (4) 1½" x 6½" rectangles

From the red-gold print, cut:
- (8) 1½" squares

Preparation

1. Read all instructions before you begin.

2. Wash, dry and press all fabrics.

3. Cutting instructions are based on 40" wide fabrics. WOF = Width of Fabric.

4. Use ¼" seams throughout.

5. Press seam allowances in the direction that allows the seams to "lock" before continuing to build each block.

6. Press all seams to the dark fabric when possible.

Build the Boot Block

Refer to the block layout.

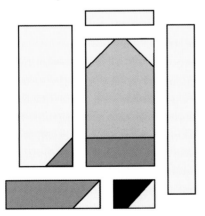

1. Draw a diagonal line, on the wrong side, on the 2" and 2½" cream squares.

2. Place the drawn-on 2" squares, with right sides together, on the top corners of the 7½" x 9½" rectangle.

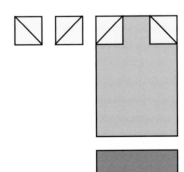

3. Sew on the drawn line. Trim, leaving a ¼" seam allowance. Open and press.

4. With right sides together, sew a 1½" x 7½" cream rectangle to the top of the boot top. Press.

5. Sew the 2½" x 7½" brown texture-print rectangle, with right sides together, to the bottom of the boot top.

6. Draw a diagonal line, on the wrong side, of the 2½" brown texture-print square.

7. Place the drawn-on square, with right sides together, on the lower right side of the 4½" x 12½" cream rectangle. Sew on the drawn line. Trim, leaving a ¼" seam allowance. Open and press.

8. With right sides together, sew the 4½" x 12½" cream rectangle to the left side. Press.

9. Place the drawn-on 2½" cream squares, with right sides together, on the right side of the 2½" x 8½" brown texture-print rectangle and the 2½" x 3½" black rectangle.

10. Sew on the drawn lines. Trim, leaving a ¼" seam allowance. Open and press.

11. With right sides together, sew the boot heel rectangle to the boot toe rectangle. Press.

12. Sew the boot bottom, with right sides together, to the boot top.

13. Sew the 1½" x 14½" cream rectangle, with right sides together, to the right side of the boot.

14. Press and set aside.

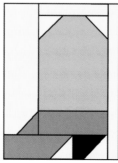

Build the Top and Bottom Units

Refer to the block layout often.

1. Sew a 1½" x 2½" gold rectangle, with right sides together, to the top and bottom of four 2½" dark blue squares.

2. With right sides together, sew another 2½" dark blue square to the bottom of each blue and gold rectangle.

3. Sew a 1½" x 6½" gold rectangle, with right sides together, to the top and bottom of two 2½" x 6½" dark blue rectangles.

4. Sew a 1½" red-gold corner square, with right sides together, to one end on four 1½" x 2½" gold rectangles. Sew the sashing sets together. Make four sets of sashing.

5. Lay out the top, center and bottom wall quilt panels as shown.

6. Sew all sections together. Press.

Finish the Quilt

Refer to the General Instructions for mitering bindings on page 13.

1. Sew the 2½" x 16½" brown border strips, with right sides together, end to end.

2. Measure the sides of the quilt. Cut the side border strips to match. Sew to the quilt top with right sides together. Repeat for the top and bottom borders.

3. Layer the quilt back (face down), batting and quilt top (face up). Baste and quilt as desired.

4. Sew the binding strips, with right sides together, end to end. Fold in half lengthwise with wrong sides together. Press.

5. Sew the raw edge on the binding to the outer edge on the wall quilt top. Miter the corners as the binding is attached.

6. Trim the backing and batting, leaving a ¼" seam allowance around the edge of the quilt.

7. Turn the folded edge of the binding to the back. Hand sew in place.

8. Sew ½" "O" rings to the top back for hanging.

RUNNER

When your hungry man sits down to the table, be prepared. This colorful quilted topper will add protection and beauty to any table or dresser. Simply change the fabric colors and make this design for any room in the home.

Finished size: 17" x 43" Dresser Topper or Table Runner

Fabrics and Notions

- ⅔ yd. dark blue print (backgrounds)
- ¾ yd. gold print (large star points, sashing, backing)
- ¼ yd. red-gold print (stars, sashing)
- ½ yd. brown leather-print (border, binding)
- ⅔ yd. batting
- Matching thread

Tools and Supplies

- Basic sewing supplies
- Rotary cutter
- Cutting mat
- Clear ruler

Cutting Instructions

From the dark blue print, cut:
- (1) 6½" x WOF strip
  From this strip, cut: (4) 2½" squares, (4) 2½" x 6½" rectangles and (1) 6½" square
- (2) 2" x WOF strip
  From these strips, cut: (8) 2" squares and (8) 2" X 3½" rectangles
- (3) 3½" x WOF strips
  From these strips, cut: (8) 3½" x 6½" rectangles and (8) 3½" squares

From the gold print, cut:
- (2) 3½" x WOF strips
  From these strips, cut: (16) 3½" squares

From the red-gold print, cut:
- (2) 3½" squares
- (1) 2" x WOF strip
  From this strip, cut: (16) 2" squares
- (1) 1½" x WOF strip
  From this strip, cut (2) 1½" x 12½" sashing strips

From the brown leather-print, cut
(6) 2½" x WOF strips (border and binding)

Preparation

1. Read all instructions before you begin.

2. Wash, dry and press all fabrics.

3. Cutting instructions are based on 40" wide fabrics. WOF = Width of Fabric.

4. Use ¼" seams throughout.

5. Press seam allowances in the direction that allows the seams to "lock" before continuing to build each block.

6. Press all seams to the dark fabric when possible.

Build the Double Star Blocks

Make two 12½" blocks

Refer to the block layout often.

1. Draw diagonal lines on the wrong side of the 3½" gold squares and the 2" red-gold squares.

2. Place a 3½" drawn-on gold square, with right sides together, on the right side of the dark blue 3½" x 6½" rectangles. Sew on the drawn line. Trim, leaving a ¼" seam allowance. Open and press.

3. Repeat, sewing the 3½" gold squares on the left side of each 3½" x 6½" dark blue rectangle. Set aside.

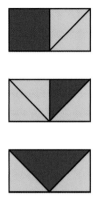

4. Place a drawn-on 2" red-gold square, with right sides together, on the right side of the 2" x 3½" dark blue rectangle. Sew on the drawn line. Trim, leaving a ¼" seam allowance. Open and press.

5. Repeat on the left side of each rectangle to make eight star point units. Press.

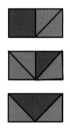

6. Lay out each block as shown on the diagram on page 93. Sew a 2" dark blue corner square, with right sides together, to the ends of the top and bottom star point units. Sew the remaining star point units to the sides of the 3½" red-gold center squares. Open and press.

7. Sew the top and bottom star point units, with right sides together, to the center star. Press.

8. Sew the gold star point units, with right sides together, to the sides of the center star.

9. Sew a 3½" dark blue square, with right sides together, to the ends of the top and bottom star point units. Press.

10. Sew the top and bottom star point units, with right sides together, to the center star. Press.

Make the Center Panel

Refer to the panel layout.

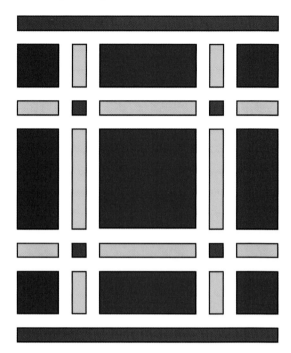

1. Sew a 1½" x 2½" gold rectangle, with right sides together, to the sides of the 2½" x 6½" dark blue rectangles.

2. Sew a 2½" dark blue square, with right sides together, to each gold rectangle end. Make two.

3. Sew a 1½" x 6½" gold rectangle, with right sides together, to the sides of the 6½" dark blue square.

4. With right sides together, sew a 2½" x 6½" dark blue rectangle to the sides of the 1½" x 6½" gold rectangles. Press.

5. With right sides together, sew a 1½" red-gold corner square to the ends of two 1½" x 6½" gold rectangles.

6. Sew a 1½" x 2½" gold rectangle, with right sides together, to each cornerstone to make two rows of sashing.

7. Lay out the top and bottom panel sections as shown.

8. Sew all the sections with right sides together. Press.

Build the Table Runner

1. Sew the 1½" red-gold sashing strips, with right sides together, to the top and bottom of the center panel.

2. Sew each of the star blocks, with right sides together, to the top and bottom of the center panel. Press.

3. Measure all the sides of the quilt. Sew the 2½" brown border strips, with right sides together, end to end. Sew the side borders, with right sides together, to the quilt. Press. Repeat for the top and bottom borders. Press.

Finish the Table Runner

Refer to the General Instructions for mitering bindings on page 13.

1. Layer the backing (face down), batting and quilt top (face up). Baste and quilt as desired. The sample shown was meander quilted.

2. Sew the 2½" brown binding strips, with right sides together, end to end. Fold in half lengthwise with wrong sides together. Press.

3. Sew the raw edge of the binding to the outer edge of the quilt top. Miter the corners as you attach the binding.

4. Trim the batting and backing fabrics, leaving a ¼" seam allowance around the runner.

5. Turn the folded edge of the binding to the back of the topper. Hand sew in place.

CHAPTER 7

Stargazing

Star quilts are great people pleasers. This collection of designs is made up of my favorite star blocks and bright-colored fabric prints. The bed quilt is enhanced by the star-block border pillowcase. The table topper also can be used as a wall or lap quilt.

Choose red, white and blue fabrics, and the set of designs will sizzle as Americana at its best. Enjoy making this beautiful galaxy collection of star projects.

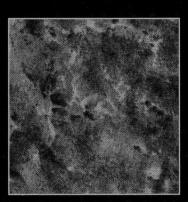

Stargazing
QUILT

Search for your favorite star, or dream of the universe beyond when cuddled under this bright cosmic quilt. Each star creates another design and the vibrant colors add a touch of energy every stargazer will love. Choose colors of fabrics like those featured in the model or consider making a two-color quilt such as cream and blue. Whatever you choose, you will find making this quilt is both fun and exciting as you create each star block.

Finished size: 69" x 93"

Fabrics and Notions
- ⅔ yd. purple print (block No. 1)
- ⅓ yd. dark blue print (block No. 1)
- ½ yd. medium yellow print (block No. 1)
- ½ yd. yellow check (block No. 2)
- ⅔ yd. medium blue print (block No. 2)
- ⅔ yd. burgundy print (block No. 3)
- ⅔ yd. red star print (block No. 3, inner border)
- ½ yd. gold print (block No. 3)
- ½ yd. yellow print (block No. 4)
- ⅓ yd. black print (block No. 4)
- ½ yd. bright blue (block No. 4)
- 1¼ yd. gold or yellow print (sashing squares, star points)
- 3½ yd. dark blue print (sashing rectangles, outer border)
- 6 yd. backing
- Full-size batting (81" x 96")
- Matching thread

Tools and Supplies
- Basic sewing supplies
- Rotary cutter
- Cutting mat
- Clear ruler

Cutting Instructions for Star Block No. 1
From the medium yellow print, cut:
- (2) 4¼" x WOF strips
  From these strips, cut: (18) 4¼" squares
- (1) 3½" x WOF strip
  From this strip, cut: (9) 3½" squares

From the purple print, cut:
- (2) 4¼" x WOF strips
  From these strips, cut: (18) 4¼" squares
- (2) 3⅞" x WOF strips
  From these strips, cut: (18) 3⅞" squares

From the dark blue print, cut:
- (2) 3⅞" x WOF strips
  From these strips, cut: (18) 3⅞" squares

Cutting Instructions for Star Block No. 2
From the yellow check, cut:
- (2) 4¼" x WOF strips
  From these strips, cut: (16) 4¼" squares
- (1) 3½" x WOF strip
  From these strips, cut: (8) 3½" squares

From the medium blue print, cut:
- (2) 4¼" x WOF strips
  From these strips, cut: (16) 4¼" squares
- (3) 3½" strips
  From these strips, cut: (32) 3½" squares

Cutting Instructions for Star Block No. 3
From the gold print, cut:
- (1) 3½" x WOF strip
  From this strip, cut: (9) 3½" squares
- (2) 3⅞" x WOF strips
  From these strips, cut: (18) 3⅞" squares

From the red star print, cut:
- (1) 4¼" x WOF strip
  From this strip, cut: (9) 4¼" squares

From the burgundy print, cut:
- (4) 3½" x WOF strips
  From these strips, cut: (36) 3½" squares
- (1) 4¼" x WOF strip
  From this strip, cut: (9) 4¼" squares

Cutting Instructions for Star Block No. 4
From the yellow print, cut:
- (1) 3½" x WOF strip
  From this strip, cut: (9) 3½" squares
- (2) 3⅞" x WOF strips
  From these strips, cut: (18) 3⅞" squares

From the black print, cut:
- (2) 3⅞" x WOF strips
  From these strips, cut: (18) 3⅞" squares

From the bright blue print, cut:
- (4) 3⅞" x WOF strips
  From these strips, cut: (36) 3⅞" squares

Cutting Instructions for Inner Border and Outer Border Cornerstones
From the red star print, cut:
- (7) 1½" x WOF strips
- (4) 5½" squares

Cutting Instructions for Outer Border, Inner Border Cornerstones, Sashing and Binding
From the dark blue print, cut:
- (15) 3½" x WOF strips
  From these strips, cut: (58) 3½" x 9½" rectangles
- (8) 5½" x WOF strips
- (4) 1½" squares
- (8) 2½" x WOF strips

Cutting Instructions for Sashing Stars
From the gold/yellow print, cut:
- (12) 2" x WOF strips
  From these strips, cut: (232) 2" squares
- (2) 3½" x WOF strips
  From these strips, cut: (24) 3½" squares

Preparation

1. Read all instructions before you begin.

2. Wash, dry and press all fabrics.

3. Cutting instructions are based on 40" wide fabrics. WOF = Width of Fabric.

4. Use ¼" seams throughout.

5. Press seam allowances in the direction that allows the seams to "lock" before continuing to build each block.

6. Press all seams to the dark fabric when possible.

Build Star Block No. 1

Make nine 9½" blocks (yellow/purple/dark blue)

1. Draw a diagonal line across the wrong side on the yellow 4¼" squares.

2. Place the purple and yellow 4¼" squares with right sides together. Sew a ¼" seam on each side of the drawn line. Cut apart on the drawn line.

3. Place the two half-square triangles, with right sides together, opposite colors touching. Draw a diagonal line across the top square.

4. Sew a ¼" seam on each side of the line. Cut apart on the drawn line. Open and press.

5. Draw a diagonal line across the wrong side on all of the 3⅞" purple squares.

6. Place the drawn-on squares, with right sides together, on the 3⅞" dark blue squares.

7. Sew a ¼" seam on each side of the drawn line. Cut on the drawn line. Open and press.

8. Lay out block No. 1 as shown below.

9. With right sides together, sew the squares together. Sew the rows together. Press and set aside.

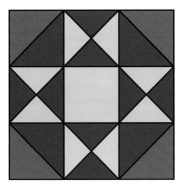

Build Star Block No. 2

Make eight 9½" blocks (yellow check/ medium blue)

1. Draw a diagonal line across the wrong side on the yellow check 4¼" squares.

2. Place the medium blue and yellow check 4¼" squares with right sides together. Sew a ¼" seam on each side of the drawn line. Cut apart on the drawn line. Open and press.

3. Place the two half-square triangles, with right sides together, opposite colors touching. Draw a diagonal line across the top square.

4. Sew a ¼" seam on each side of the line. Cut apart on the drawn line. Open and press.

5. Lay out block No. 2 as shown.

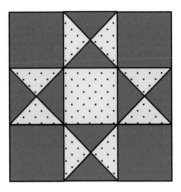

6. With right sides together, sew the squares together. With right sides together, sew the rows together.

7. Press. Set aside.

Build Star Block No. 3

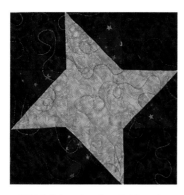

Make nine 9½" blocks (gold/red star/ burgundy)

1. Draw a diagonal line across the wrong side on the 4¼" red star squares and the 3⅞" gold squares.

2. Place the burgundy and red star 4¼" squares with right sides together.

3. Sew a ¼" seam on each side of the drawn line. Cut apart on the drawn line. Open and press.

4. Place the burgundy and red star half-square triangles, right sides together, on the 3⅞" gold squares.

5. Sew a ¼" seam on each side of the line on the gold squares. Cut apart on the drawn line. Open and press.

6. Lay out block No. 3 as shown. (The star points on four blocks will be the mirror image of the remaining four blocks.)

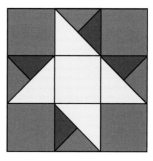

7. With right sides together, sew the squares together. With right sides together, sew the rows together. Press and set aside.

Build Star Block No. 4

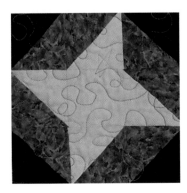

Make nine 9½" blocks (black/yellow/bright blue)

1. Draw a diagonal line across the wrong side of the yellow 3⅞" squares.

2. Place the bright blue and yellow 3⅞" squares with right sides together. Sew a ¼" seam on each side of the drawn line.

3. Cut apart on the drawn line. Open and press.

4. Draw a diagonal line across the wrong side on the 3⅞" bright blue squares.

5. Place the bright blue 3⅞" squares, with right sides together, on the black 3⅞" squares.

6. Sew a ¼" seam on each side of the drawn line. Cut apart on the drawn line. Open and press.

7. Lay out block No. 4 as shown.

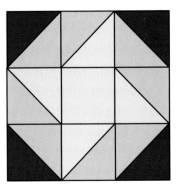

8. With right sides together, sew the squares together. With right sides together, sew the rows together. Press and set aside.

Make the Sashing

1. Draw a diagonal line across the wrong side of all the 2" yellow squares.

2. Place a drawn-on square, with right sides together, on the lower left hand and upper right hand side on each 3½" x 9½" dark blue rectangle.

3. Sew on the drawn lines.

4. Trim, leaving a ¼" seam allowance. Open and press.

5. Repeat Step 2 on the lower right and upper left corners.

6. Trim, open and press.

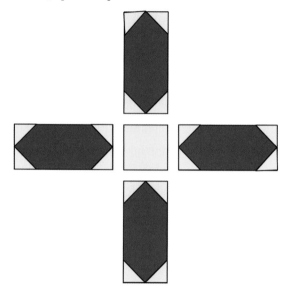

Build the Quilt

Refer to the quilt photo often.

1. Place the quilt blocks and sashing units as shown.

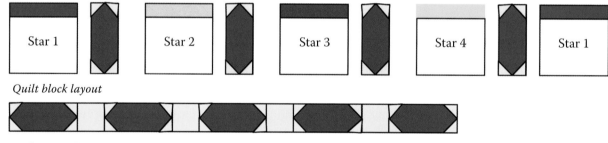

Quilt block layout

Sashing row layout

2. Sew the blocks, with right sides together, to make seven rows of five blocks. Press.

3. Sew five sashing units, with right sides together, to four 3½" yellow squares to make one row of sashing. Continue to make a total of six sashing rows.

4. With right sides together, sew the rows of star blocks to the sashing rows.

5. Sew the 1½" red star border strips, with right sides together, end to end. Measure the sides of the quilt. Cut the side borders to match. Sew the side borders to the quilt with rights sides together.

6. Measure the top and bottom borders. Sew a 1½" dark blue cornerstone square, with right sides together, to the ends of the top and bottom borders.

7. Sew the top and bottom inner border to the quilt, with right sides together.

8. Piece and sew the 5½" dark blue outer border strips, with right sides together, end to end. Measure all sides of the quilt. Cut the side borders to match. Sew the side borders to the quilt with right sides together.

9. Cut the top and bottom blue border strips to match.

10. Sew a 5½" red star cornerstone, with right sides together, to the ends on the top and bottom borders. Press.

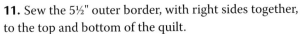

11. Sew the 5½" outer border, with right sides together, to the top and bottom of the quilt.

Finish The Quilt

1. Layer the backing (face down), batting and quilt top (face up). Baste and quilt as desired. The model was quilted using a meander and loopy-star motif.

2. Sew the binding strips, with right sides together, end to end. Fold in half lengthwise with wrong sides together. Press.

3. Sew the raw edge of the binding to the outer edge of the quilt top.

4. Trim the quilt backing fabric and batting, leaving a scant ¼" seam allowance around the edge of the quilt.

5. Turn the folded edge of the binding to the back of the quilt. Hand sew in place.

Stargazing
TABLE TOPPER

This quilted table topper or wall hanging makes an excellent topper for a patio table as you enjoy a candlelight dinner, or as a wall hanging in the den or family room. The squares stabilize the quilt, while the stars accent the dark background. It also makes a great, little picnic quilt to take to the lake and enjoy the fireworks with your favorite fellow.

Finished size: 45" square

Fabrics and Notions

- 2 yd. dark blue print (background, stars)
- ½ yd. yellow (star blocks)
- ½ yd. red star print (binding)
- 2⅔ yd. backing
- 2⅔ yd. batting
- Matching thread

Tools and Supplies

- Basic sewing supplies
- Cutting mat
- Clear ruler
- Rotary cutter

Cutting Instructions

From the dark blue print, cut:
- (5) 9½" x WOF strips
  From these strips, cut: (17) 9½" squares
- (3) 3½" x WOF strips
  From these strips, cut: (32) 3½" squares
- (2) 4¼" x WOF strips
  From these strips, cut: (16) 4¼" squares

From the yellow print, cut:
- (1) 3½" x WOF strip
  From this strip, cut: (8) 3½" squares
- (2) 4¼" x WOF strips
  From these strips, cut: (16) 4¼" squares

From the red star print, cut:
- (5) 2½" x WOF strips

Preparation

1. Read all instructions before you begin.

2. Wash, dry and press all fabrics.

3. Cutting instructions are based on 40" wide fabrics.
WOF = Width of Fabric.

4. Use ¼" seams throughout.

5. Press seam allowances in the direction that allows the seams to "lock" before continuing to build each block.

6. Press all seams to the dark fabric when possible.

Build the Star Blocks

Make eight 9½" star blocks

1. Draw a diagonal line across the wrong side on the 4¼" yellow print squares.

2. Place the drawn-on yellow squares, with right sides together, on the 4¼" dark blue squares.

3. Sew a ¼" seam on each side of the drawn line. Cut apart on the drawn line. Open and press.

Make 32 half-square triangle blocks

4. Place two of the half-square triangle blocks together with opposite colors touching. Draw a diagonal line across the wrong side on the top square. Sew a ¼" seam on each side of the drawn line. Cut apart on the drawn line. Open and press.

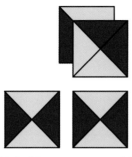

Make 32 quarter-square blocks.

5. Lay out the star block as shown.

6. Sew the squares for each row together. Press. Sew the rows together to make a star block. Make eight 9½" star blocks.

Build the Table Topper

1. Lay out the quilt in rows, using the nine star blocks and the (17) blue 9½" squares. Sew all blocks with right sides together.

2. Row 1: One star block, three blue blocks and one star block.
Row 2: One blue block, one star block, one blue block, one star block and one blue block.
Row 3: Five blue blocks
Row 4: One blue block, one star block, one blue block, one star block and one blue block.
Row 5: One star block, three blue blocks and one star block.

3. Sew the rows together. Press.

Finish the Table Topper

Refer to the General Instructions for mitering bindings on page 13.

1. Layer the backing (face down), batting and quilt top (face up). Baste and quilt as desired. The model was quilted using an overall meander and star-loop motif.

2. Sew the red star 2½" x WOF binding strips, with right sides together, end to end. Fold in half lengthwise with wrong sides together. Press.

3. Sew the raw edge of the binding to the outer edge of the quilt top.

4. Trim the batting and backing, leaving ¼" seam allowance around the outer edge of the quilt.

5. Turn the folded edge of the binding to the back of the quilt. Hand sew in place.

Stargazing
PILLOWCASE

This very stylish pillowcase is easy to create. The star blocks give the pillowcase edge a dramatic look and there's no need for additional pillow shams when you place this pillowcase on your bed.

Finished size: 20" x 34

Fabrics and Notions

- 1¼ yd. dark blue print (pillowcase body, star block background)
- ¼ yd. red print (pillowcase cuff, edge lining
- ¼ yd. yellow print (star blocks)
- Matching thread

Tools and Supplies

- Basic sewing supplies
- Cutting mat
- Clear ruler
- Rotary cutter

Cutting Instructions

From the dark blue print, cut:
- (1) 27½" x 41" rectangle
- (5) 2" x WOF strips
  From these strips, cut: (24) 2" x 3½" rectangles and (24) 2" squares
- (1) 1½" x WOF strip
  From this strip, cut: (5) 1½" x 6½" rectangles

From the yellow print, cut:
- (1) 3-1/2" x WOF strip
  From this strip, cut: (6) 3½" squares
- (3) 2" x WOF strips
  From these strips, cut: (48) 2" squares

From the red print, cut:
- (1) 7" x WOF strip
- (1) 2½" x WOF strip

Preparation

1. Read all instructions before you begin.

2. Wash, dry and press all fabrics.

3. Cutting instructions are based on 40" wide fabrics. WOF = Width of Fabric.

4. Use ¼" seams throughout.

5. Press seam allowances in the direction that allows the seams to "lock" before continuing to build each block.

6. Press all seams to the dark fabric when possible.

Make the Pillowcase

1. Fold the 2½" x WOF red strip in half lengthwise with wrong sides together. Press.

2. Pin the raw edge of the red folded strip on top of the 41" raw edge on the 27½" x 41" blue rectangle.

3. Trim the red strip to the edge. Sew in place using a ¼" seam. Set aside.

Build the Star Blocks

(Make six blocks)

1. Draw a diagonal line across the wrong side on all of the 2" yellow squares.

2. Place a drawn-on 2" yellow square, with right sides together, on the right side of a 2" x 3½" dark blue rectangle. Sew on the drawn line. Trim, leaving a ¼" seam allowance. Open and press.

3. Repeat on the left side of the rectangle. Press. Make 24 star point units.

4. Place each blue 2" square and the star point unit blocks as shown on the diagram.

5. Sew a 2" dark blue corner square, with right sides together, to the ends of the top and bottom star point units. Sew the remaining star point units to the sides of the 3½" yellow center squares. Open and press. Sew the top and bottom star point units to the center square. Press.

6. Lay out the pillowcase edge as shown in the pillowcase photo on page 111.

7. Sew the 1½" x 6½" dark blue rectangles, with right sides together, between the star blocks. Press.

Build the Pillowcase

1. With right sides together, sew the star block row to the top edge of the pillowcase on top of the red star strip. Press.

2. Fold the pillowcase in half with right sides together.

3. Sew the side and bottom seams.

4. Turn right-side out.

5. Fold the 7" x 41" red star print in half, with right sides together, meeting the 7" ends. Sew the side seam.

6. With right sides together, sew the red lining to the top edge of the pillowcase. Press.

7. Turn the lining to the inside. Turn the bottom of the lining under ¼" to ½". Hand sew in place, covering the seam.

CHAPTER 8

Wildwood Lodge

It isn't even necessary to take a walk in the woods when you decorate a bedroom with this wonderful, warm flannel quilt and mantel cover. Use the mantel cover for a dresser topper if you don't have a fireplace. Just dream of hiking and fishing trips or grand hunting excursions when you sleep under this beauty.

Wildwood Lodge QUILT

Step into a room or cabin hideaway filled with this lodge-look quilt and you will feel right at home. The rich, deep colors of flannel set off the lighter prints. The large Bear's Paw blocks anchor the center panel. Strip-pieced tile blocks are used to create the center panel and border. Overall quilting completes this large, fabulous quilt.

Finished size: 88" x 100"

Fabrics and Notions

- 3½ yd. cream-green print flannel (center blocks, large and small Bear's Paw blocks)
- 2 yd. brown check flannel (sashing, large and small Bear's Paw blocks)
- 1⅛ yd. black-brown print flannel (large and small Bear's Paw blocks, border blocks, cornerstones, binding)
- 1¾ yd. green print flannel (block center squares, outer border
- 2 yd. tan print flannel (outer border blocks)
- 1 yd. cream print flannel (outer border sashing)
- 8¼ yd. backing flannel
- Queen-size batting (90" x 108")

Tools and Supplies

- Basic sewing supplies
- Rotary cutter
- Cutting mat
- Clear ruler

Cutting Instructions

From the cream-green print, cut:
- (16) 5½" x WOF strips
- (1) 3½" x WOF strip
  From this strip, cut: (4) 3½" squares
- (2) 3⅞" x WOF strips
  From these strips, cut: (12) 3⅞" squares
- (2) 1½" x WOF strips
  From these strips, cut: (4) 1½" x 8½" rectangles and (4) 1½" x 9½" rectangles
- (2) 2½" x WOF strips
  From these strips, cut: (4) 2½" squares, (4) 2½" x 4½" rectangles and (4) 2½" x 6½" rectangles
- (3) 2⅞ " x WOF strips
  From these strips, cut: (32) 2⅞" squares

From the brown check, cut:
- (2) 3⅞" x WOF strips
  From these strips, cut: (12) 3⅞" squares
- (9) 2½" x WOF strips
  From one of these strips, cut: (4) 2½" squares and (4) 2½" x 4½" rectangles
  Note: The remaining strips will be used for the center blocks.
- (4) 5½" x WOF strips
- (1) 4½" strip
  From this strip, cut: (4) 4½" squares

From the black-brown print, cut:
- (3) 2⅞" x WOF strips
  From these strips, cut: (32) 2⅞" squares
- (9) 2½" x WOF strips
  From one strip, cut: (4) 2½" squares
  Note: The remaining strips will be used for binding.
- (2) 1½" x WOF strips

From the green print, cut:
- (2) 2½" x WOF strips
- (8) 6½" x WOF strips

From the tan print, cut:
- (16) 4" x WOF strips
- (1) 2½" strip
  From this strip, cut: (8) 2½" squares

From the cream print, cut:
- (8) 1½" x WOF strips
- (4) 4" x WOF strips

Preparation

1. Read all instructions before you begin.

2. Wash, dry and press all fabrics.

3. Cutting instructions are based on 40" wide fabrics. WOF = Width of Fabric.

4. Use ¼" seams throughout.

5. Press seam allowances in the direction that allows the seams to "lock" before continuing to build each block.

6. Press all seams to the dark fabric when possible.

Build the Large Bear's Paw Blocks
Make four 12½" blocks

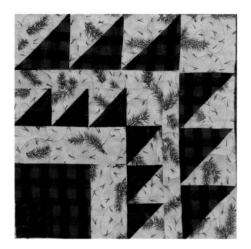

1. Draw a diagonal line across the wrong side on the 12 cream-green 3⅞" squares and the 32 cream-green 2⅞" squares. The large Bear's Paw block will use 12 of the 2⅞" squares. Set the others to the side.

2. With right sides together, place the drawn-on cream-green 3⅞" squares on the 3⅞" brown check squares. Sew a ¼" seam on each side of the drawn line. Cut apart on the drawn line. Open and press.

3. With right sides together, place the drawn-on 2⅞" cream-green squares on the 2⅞" brown-black squares. Sew a ¼" seam on each side of the drawn-on line.

4. Cut apart on the drawn line. Open and press. Set aside. The 24 half-square triangle 2½" blocks will be used on the large Bear's Paw blocks.

5. With right sides together, sew the 2½" black-brown square to the 2½" brown check square. Make four.

6. With right sides together, sew the 2½" x 4½" brown check rectangle to the squares. Make four.

7. With right sides together, sew a cream-green 2½" x 4½" rectangle to the four brown check 4½" rectangle sides. Press.

8. With right sides together, sew the cream-green 2½" x 6½" rectangles to the top on each unit.

9. Refer to the block drawing on page 119. Sew together eight sets of three 2½" half-square triangle blocks. Press.

10. With right sides together, sew a 2½" cream-green square to the end of four three half-square triangle block sections. Press.

11. Place a three half-square triangle block section, with right sides together, on the right side of each of the center units. Sew in place. Press.

12. With right sides together, sew the half-square triangle block sections, with the cream-green square attached, to the center units. Press to complete the four units.

13. With right sides together, sew a 1½" x 8½" cream rectangle to the right side of each unit. Press.

14. With right sides together, sew a 1½" x 9½" cream rectangle to the top of each unit. Press.

15. Refer to the block drawing. Sew together eight sets of three 3½" half-square-triangle blocks.

16. Place a 3½" cream-green square, with right sides together, on the ends of four half-square-triangle block sections. Sew in place. Open and press.

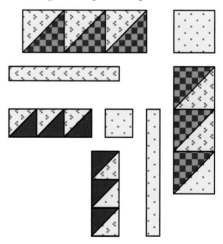

17. Sew a three half-square triangle block section, with right sides together, on the right side of each unit. Press.

18. With right sides together, sew the three half-square triangle block sections, with the cream-green square attached, to the top of each unit to complete the block. Press.

19. Set the four large Bear's Paw blocks to the side.

Build the Small Bear's Paw Border Blocks

Make four 8½" border blocks.

1. The remaining 2½" half-square triangles, from Step No. 1 under the large Bear's Paw block instructions, are used for the small Bear's Paw blocks. Build the blocks referring to the diagram shown. Sew all seams with right sides together.

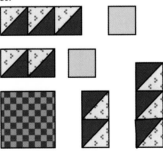

2. Sew together four sets of two half-square triangle blocks. Sew together four sets of three half-square triangle blocks. Press.

3. Sew a 2½" tan square to the end of four of the two half-square triangle block sections.

4. Sew a 2½" tan square to the end of four of the three half-square triangle block sections.

5. Sew a two half-square triangle block section to the right side on each of the 4½" brown check squares. Press.

6. Sew a two half-square triangle block section, with the tan square attached, to the top on each brown check and two half-square triangle unit.

7. Sew a three half-square triangle block section to the right side of each unit.

8. To complete the small Bear's Paw blocks, sew a three half-square triangle block section, with the 2½" tan square attached, to the top of each block.

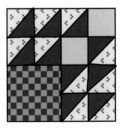

Build the Quilt Center Tile Blocks
Make (26) 12½" blocks

1. With right sides together, sew a brown check 2½" x WOF strip to one side of a 5½" x WOF cream-green strip. Press.

2. With right sides together, sew another cream-green 5½" x WOF strip to the opposite side on the brown check 2½" x WOF strip. Make eight strip sets.

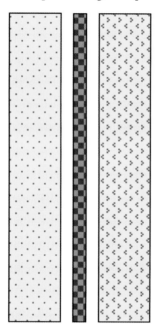

3. Cut the eight strip sets into (52) 5½" x 12½" segments. Set aside.

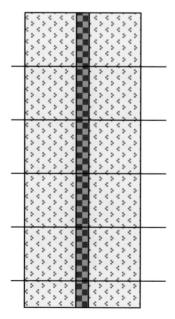

4. With right sides together, sew a brown check 5½" x WOF strip to each side of a 2½" x WOF green strip. Make two strip sets.

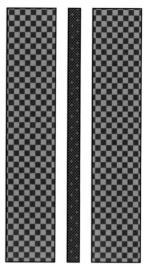

5. Cut the two strip sets into (26) 2½" x 12½" segments.

6. Lay out the block as shown.

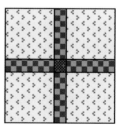

7. With right sides together, sew a 5½" x 12½" segment to both sides of the 2½" x 12½" segment. Press. Make 26 blocks.

Build the Quilt Center

Refer to the quilt diagram for placement.

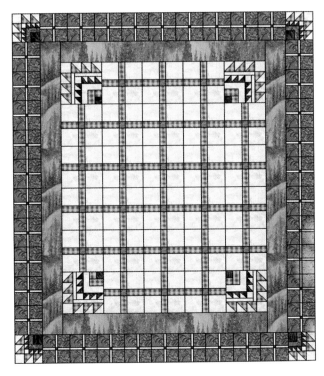

1. With right sides together, sew the five blocks together to make each row. Press.

2. With right sides together, sew the six rows together. Press.

Build the Borders

1. Sew the 6½" green border strips, with right sides together, end to end.

2. Measure all sides of the quilt. Cut the needed lengths for the top and bottom borders. Sew in place with right sides together. Repeat for the side borders.

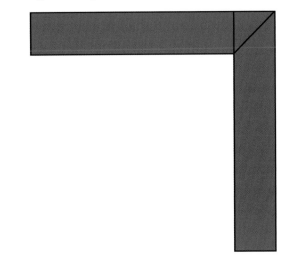

Build the Border Tile Blocks
Make (38) 8½" tile blocks plus two segments

1. With right sides together, sew a tan 4" x WOF strip to the sides of a cream 1½" x WOF strip. Make eight strip sets.

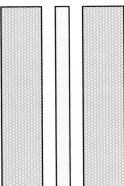

2. Cut these strip sets into (76) 4" x 8½" segments. Cut two 6½" x 8½" segments.

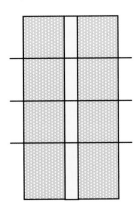

3. With right sides together, sew a cream 4" x WOF strip to each side of the brown-black 1½" x WOF strip. Make two strip sets.

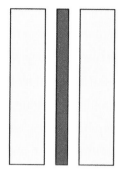

4. Cut these two strip sets into (38) 1½" x 8½" segments.

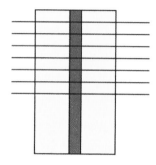

5. With right sides together, sew a tan/cream 4" x 8½" segment to each side of the cream and brown-black 1½" x 8½ segment. Make 38 blocks.

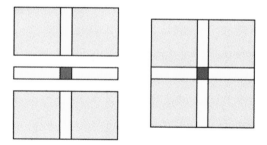

6. Sew two sets of nine block rows, with right sides together, to make the top and bottom borders.

7. Sew two sets of ten block rows plus one segment, with right sides together, to make the side borders.

8. With right sides together, sew the side borders in place. Trim to fit.

9. Sew a small Bear's Paw block to both ends of the top and bottom borders with right sides together.

10. Sew the top and bottom borders in place with right sides together. Press.

Finish the Quilt

Refer to the General Instructions for mitering bindings on page 13.

1. Cut and sew the backing fabric 3" larger than the quilt top.

2. Layer the backing (face down), batting and quilt top (face up). Baste and quilt as desired. An overall meander quilting technique was used on the model.

3. Sew the 2½" binding strips, with right sides together, end to end.

4. Fold in half lengthwise with wrong sides together. Press.

5. Sew the raw edge of the binding to the outer edge of the quilt top.

6. Trim the backing fabric and batting, leaving ¼" seam allowance around the quilt edge.

7. Turn the folded edge of the binding to the back of the quilt. Hand sew in place.

Bear's Paw
MANTELCOVER

Small Bear's Paw and tile blocks were used to construct this woodsy mantel cover or dresser topper. The easy-to-make topper adds an earthy lodge look to any home.

Finished size: 16" x 40"

Fabrics and Notions

- ¼ yd. cream-green print flannel (Bear's Paw blocks)
- ½ yd. tan print flannel (sashing blocks)
- ¼ yd. brown check flannel (Bear's Paw blocks)
- ½ yd. brown-black print flannel (Bear's Paw blocks, center squares, binding)
- ⅓ yd. cream print flannel (block sashings)
- ⅔ yd. flannel backing
- ⅔ yd. batting

Tools and Supplies

- Basic sewing supplies
- Rotary cutter
- Cutting mat
- Clear ruler

Cutting Instructions

From the cream-green print, cut:
- (1) 2½" x WOF strip
  From this strip, cut: (4) 2½" squares
- (1) 2⅞" x WOF strip
  From this strip, cut: (10) 2⅞" squares

From the black-brown print, cut:
- (1) 2⅞" x WOF strip
  From this strip, cut: (10) 2⅞" squares
- (1) 1½" x WOF strip
- (3) 2½" x WOF strips

From the tan print, cut:
- (4) 4" x WOF strips

From the cream print, cut:
- (2) 1½" x WOF strips
- (2) 4" x WOF strips

Preparation

1. Read all instructions before you begin.

2. Wash, dry and press all fabrics.

3. Cutting instructions are based on 40" wide fabrics. WOF = Width of Fabric.

4. Use ¼" seams throughout.

5. Press seam allowances in the direction that allows the seams to "lock" before continuing to build each block.

6. Press all seams to the dark fabric when possible.

Build the Bear's Paw Border Blocks

Make two 8½" blocks

1. Draw a diagonal line across the wrong side on the 2⅞" cream-green squares.

2. With right sides together, place the drawn-on squares on the 2⅞" black-brown squares.

3. Sew a ¼" seam on each side of the drawn line. Cut apart on the drawn line. Open and press.

4. Lay out the small Bear's Paw block as shown.

5. Sew four sets of two half-square triangle blocks with right sides together.

6. Sew four sets of three half-square triangle blocks with right sides together.

7. Sew a 2½" cream-green square, with right sides together, to the end of two half-square triangle block sections.

8. Sew a 2½" tan square, with right sides together, to the end of two three half-square triangle block sections.

9. With right sides together, sew a two half-square triangle block section to the right side of each 4½" brown check square. Press.

10. Sew a two half-square triangle block section, with the 2½" cream-green square attached, to the top of each brown check square and two half-square triangle block unit.

11. With right sides together, sew a three half-square triangle block section to the right side of each unit.

12. To complete the blocks, sew a three half-square triangle block section, with the tan square attached, to the top of each block.

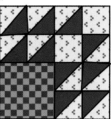

Build the Tile Blocks
Make eight 8½" blocks

1. With right sides together, sew a tan 4" x WOF strip to the both sides of a cream 1½" x WOF cream strip. Make two strip sets.

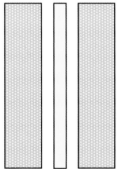

2. Cut these two strip sets into (16) 4" x 8½" segments.

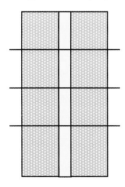

3. With right sides together, sew a cream 4" x WOF strip to the both sides of the brown-black 1½" x WOF strip.

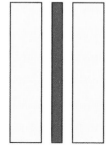

4. Cut this unit into eight 1½" x 8½" segments.

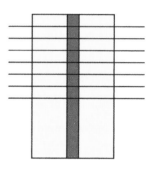

5. With right sides together, sew a 4" x 8½" segment to the sides of the 1½" x 8½" segment. Make eight blocks.

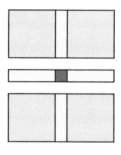

Make eight blocks

6. Refer to the quilt photo.

7. Sew a row of five tile blocks, with right sides together. Sew a row of three tile blocks with right sides together.

8. Sew a small Bear's Paw block, with right sides together, to each end of the three block row.

9. Sew the two rows together. Press.

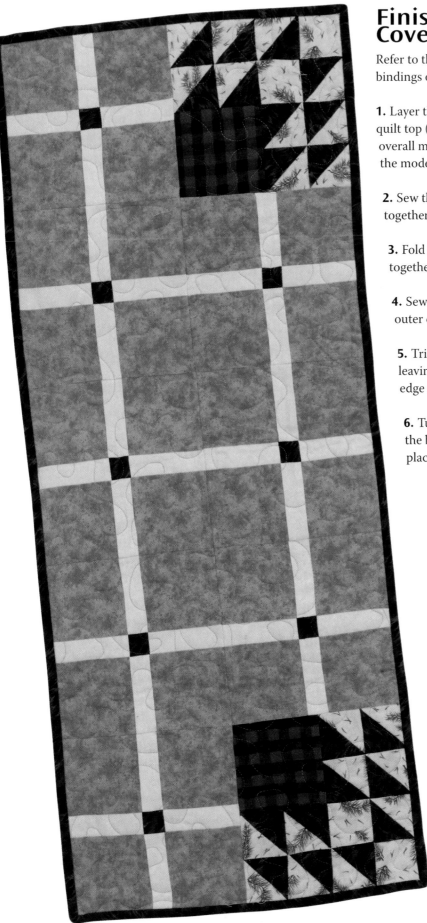

Finish the Mantel Cover

Refer to the General Instructions for mitering bindings on page 13.

1. Layer the backing (face down), batting and quilt top (face up). Baste and quilt as desired. An overall meander quilting technique was used on the model.

2. Sew the 2½" binding strips, with right sides together, end to end.

3. Fold in half lengthwise with wrong sides together. Press.

4. Sew the raw edge of the binding to the outer edge of the mantel cover.

5. Trim off the backing fabric and binding, leaving a ¼" seam allowance around the edge of the mantel cover.

6. Turn the folded edge of the binding to the back of the mantel cover. Hand sew in place.

Resources

Troy Corporation
2701 N. Normandy Ave.
Chicago, IL 60707
(800) 888-2400
Fabrics

The Warm Company
954 East Union St.
Seattle, WA 98122
(800) 234-WARM
http://www.warmcompany.com
Steam-a-Seam Lite 2

S.A. Richards, Inc.
P.O. Box 1037
Fort Lee, NJ 07024
(201) 947-3850
E-mail: sarichards@earthlink.net
SAR® Fat quarter organizer

The following companies and contributors generously provided their locations and/or items for the photos in this book.

Glacier Wood Golf Club of Iola
604 Water St.
Iola, WI 54945
(715) 445-3831

Rosholt Motorcycle Club
207 N. Main St.
Rosholt, WI 54473
(715) 677-4738
rmotorco@wi-net.com

Stu's Home Interiors
914 Furman Drive
Waupaca, WI 54981
(800) 657-6933

Hansen Brand Source
990 W. Fulton St.
Waupaca, WI 54981
(800) 773-4746
http://www.homeappliances.com/Hansen

Rosholt High School

Joe and Tricia Kertzman

Bob and Judi Brooks

John Gunnell

Brian Earnest